Bristol Radical Pa

Conflict and Struggle in the Arms Industry

A Memoir of a Bristol Trade Union Activist

Andy Danford

ISBN 978-1-911522-65-2

Bristol Radical History Group. 2022.
www.brh.org.uk
brh@brh.org.uk

Contents

Introduction—v

1969-1973: Early years as an engineering apprentice—1

1974-1979: British Aircraft Corporation and BICC—16

1979-1987: British Aerospace, before the job losses—32

1988-1991: The jobs crisis—86

1990: Human Resource Management—109

Epilogue—121

Abbreviations—123

Bibliography—125

Acknowledgements—126

BAe bombshell

By Michael Bimpson

Workers in shock as 1,300 jobs are axed

Andy Danford

SHOCK and disbelief stunned some of Bristol's — and Britain's — best brains yesterday.

The message that they were no longer needed to equip the armed forces came only weeks after the world saw the deadly accuracy of the missiles they designed.

Of the 2,100 who packed an assembly room at British Aerospace's Dynamics company in Filton yesterday, 1,300 face being out of a job by the year-end.

Joining the growing ranks of unemployed is the reward for some who gave up Christmas holidays and put in extra overtime to aid the Gulf War effort.

Prospects

Their ALARM, Sea Skua and Sea Dart missiles helped destroy Iraq's forces and defend Allied ships in the 43-day Gulf War.

Many are highly-skilled graduates and some earn salaries of around £20,000 a year.

Now prospects for finding new jobs, let alone ones at comparable rates of pay, are dim.

Jeremy Smallwood

Louise Cordy

Emma Robbins

Derek Perkins

BAe Bombshell, *Evening Post*, **21st March 1991.**

Introduction

In the spring of 1991, British Aerospace announced a third wave of mass redundancies in almost as many years at its Filton Naval Weapons Division. As a result, a factory that had previously employed 4,700 skilled workers was reduced to a rump of just 600 specialist staff. I lost my job in this redundancy. I also lost my life as a full-time union representative and peace campaigner of sorts. I use the latter term in the sense that I led a trade union fight for arms conversion, that is, converting the plant's output from weapons to socially useful products.

There exists an immense amount of published work in academia on industrial relations in the UK and how this has changed over time from the period of early industrialisation to the present day. Much of this comprises fairly dry accounts of the nature of management-union relationships. An insufficient attempt is made to describe the lived experiences of those who have laboured on the shop and office floors of British workplaces, or, indeed, of the union activists who have represented them. There are a good number of biographies describing the lives of various notable industrialists, senior managers and trade union leaders but wherever rank and file activists are mentioned in these accounts they are a secondary concern and too often treated in pejorative terms. My memoir does mention certain industrialists, corporate managers, union leaders and both national and local politicians, but its central focus is on rank-and-file trade union members and their elected shop stewards and union representatives. I would argue that this 'history from below' perspective provides a richer account of the reality of industrial relations in all its complexity at the workplace level.

I have placed this memoir of my life as a union activist in a personal historical context. I begin my story from the date I left school and entered the engineering industry as an apprentice in 1969. This is necessary because these were important formative years for both my understanding of workplace politics and trade unionism and for my life as a young adult and parent. It ends in the summer of 1991 when I was made redundant. The intervening years covered a period in British industrial relations when the balance of power between employers and trade unions shifted dramatically in favour of the former. The decade of the 1970s has often been described as a golden age for trade unions. Membership grew steadily to a peak of over 13 million in 1979 and in the sectors where trade unionism was particularly strong, such as manufacturing, workplace unions were able to exert a good deal of control over the management of their members' work, including how it was conducted, its content and the pace and intensity of work, along with wages and conditions of employment. As an aerospace shop-floor worker at this time, I provide plentiful observations and recollections of this union strength at my plant.

In 1979, I became a white-collar worker, moving from the shop floor to a design support role. It was not long before I became an activist with the engineering union AUEW-TASS and steadily progressed to a position of senior representative (or union convenor). This coincided with the election of Margaret Thatcher's Conservative government and the growing dominance of the ideology of Thatcherism notable for its support of privatisation, its rejection of the idea of a welfare state and, of course, its attacks on trade unionism and collectivism. These new political conditions formed the stark background for much of my trade union activity detailed in this memoir. I became deeply involved in a struggle not merely for better wages and conditions but eventually for rank-and-file control over what products workers produce and how they produce them.

Inevitably, and especially for the earlier years, I have to rely to an extent on memory though, in a few instances, with the aid of references to other sources. In some cases, my recollections are vivid and in others less precise in terms of dates. In the later years, specifically, from the mid-1980s onwards, my memories are supported by documentation such as detailed union newsletters and correspondence, local authority material and a good collection of newspaper reports.

1969-1973: Early years as an engineering apprentice

1969: Leaving school

I left school in the summer of 1969 clutching a plastic bag handed to all boy leavers. Swindon Borough Council's education department had decided to prepare me for adulthood by packing it with various items such as a comb, shaving materials and a packet of condoms. I do not know what the girls received. Commonweal Comprehensive, which had been a grammar school when I arrived in 1966 from another grammar, Saint Bonaventure's in Forest Gate, east London, converted in 1967 following the drive to massively expand comprehensive education by Anthony Crosland, the Labour Secretary of State for Education. All I can remember of this process as a schoolboy was witnessing the large influx of new boys and girls from two different secondary modern schools in the town. And of course, some of them were very clever. One, Michael Hawkins, joined my circle of friends at the time, and is currently Professor of Epidemiology and Director of the Centre for Childhood Cancer Survivor Studies at the University of Birmingham. I mention this as a small reminder of the crass injustice and dysfunction of the 11-plus examination system and the grammar school-secondary modern divide.

I managed to get seven GCE O-levels after a couple of resits. I have to admit I was not the best behaved or committed of pupils. For one, I had come to resent authority as I matured in my teens and seemed to develop an unwarranted dislike of schoolteachers. Perhaps this arose from my experience of school in London. Saint Bonaventure's was marked by a highly disciplined, bullying culture. Kids were generally scared of the bigger boys in the years above them, newly arrived boys from the West Indies were regularly set upon by the school bullies and some of the schoolteachers themselves suffered breakdowns as a result of physical or psychological torment by certain pupils. Others dished out the cane quite liberally, the worst being the appropriately named Latin teacher, Mr Kilboy. Any misdeed might result in Mr Kilboy instructing the poor pupil to walk to the staff common room to request the longest cane. Once in Kilboy's hands the pupil would receive six of the best. I suffered this. It was a rite of passage for most boys. I was not happy there. Indeed, when in the autumn of 1965 I told the small number of my class friends that I would be moving to Swindon in the summer of '66 I was abruptly 'sent to Coventry'. Thus the last two terms of my schooling there were truly uncomfortable.

During the 1960s, large numbers of businesses (and families) located in the East End moved out of the city to greater London suburbia (especially Essex) and to new towns such as Swindon. My father's employer (Sharp Perrin, a clothing and textiles business) was one of these. Swindon was not a new town as such, it was an old engineering town, but with the new migrations it was planning significant expansion.

When I arrived at Commonweal School, I encountered a new experience. Located right on the edge of town with the fields and low hills of northern Wiltshire on its doorstep, I discovered a more relaxed atmosphere where, if pupils didn't behave or toe the line, the most you could expect was a mild ticking off or a detention, never the cane. I made many new friends and, in some respects, initially at least, I was looked up to because I was the kid from London who supported West Ham United (three of their players had just won the World Cup) and who loved the new sounds of Stax R&B and Jamaican blue beat. I had picked this up from listening to the music that belted out of the growing number of West Indian house parties around our streets in Manor Park, East Ham, where my family lived. Later on, some of these came to be called 'blues' clubs. Along with the sense of youth liberation, which was emerging during the mid-1960s, my new status gave me a sense of freedom and indeed cockiness if I'm honest. The result was that I didn't really apply myself diligently to study at school. Apart from a single A grade in Biology my O-level grades were mostly mid-range. My attitude was best summed up by my form master Mr R. Cook's end of term report in December 1966: "He seems to have ability but is not using it to the full. He has collected too many detentions for his conduct to be entirely satisfactory."

Nevertheless, with enough O-Level passes I could have stayed on at school to study A-levels. My elder brother Mike had followed this path and he eventually went to Cardiff University to study town and country planning. But there existed no expectation from my parents that I should do the same. They were probably influenced by my constant stream of disappointing school reports. My elder sister Margaret did not go to university either. She led a fairly high-spirited life as a teenager in London, having various boyfriends who were scooter riding mods. She would regularly come home in the early hours to argue with my angry father after nights out at the West End discos such as the Marquee and Tiles. She greatly resented having to move to Swindon and within a couple of years became pregnant and married her first husband Ian. With all this going on, I slipped under my parents' radar and was more or less left to myself to decide my immediate future. And the problem was I didn't really know what I wanted to do with my life. In the months leading up to leaving school I visited its careers officer once or twice. This man advised me that boys in my position in Swindon would conventionally enter an apprenticeship with one of the local large engineering firms. So that's precisely what I did.

In Swindon at that time, there were four large engineering employers: British Rail Engineering, Plesseys, Pressed Steel Fisher (later to become part of British Leyland) and Vickers Armstrongs. Being awkward, I decided to go for none of these. Instead, and following my interest in sporty cars, which probably stemmed from my interest in Grand Prix motor racing as a young boy (an interest which I'm relieved to say I no longer have), I decided to apply to the MG sports car works at Cowley. I subsequently attended a strange job interview, strange because I was accompanied by my mother! The Personnel Department probably advised this because, had I got the job, I would have had to live close by the plant in digs at the age of 17 and perhaps they wanted evidence of parental support. I don't think I realised this at the time, assuming that I could hop on to a bus for a pleasant arcadian daily commute, and when the reality sunk in, I shied away at the prospect.

So, back to the big four at Swindon, I then went for an interview at Vickers Armstrongs and was offered a technician apprenticeship which I duly accepted. I started in the autumn of 1969 and, I have to say, this was one of the happiest periods of my life. I realise now that these types of apprenticeships were not just gateways to acquiring various technical skills, they also provided the means of assimilation into manhood.

1969-1973: An apprenticeship at Vickers Armstrongs

Vickers Armstrongs was a major shipbuilding, aircraft and military hardware designer and manufacturer with large plants on Tyneside, at Barrow in Furness and at Leeds. The Swindon plant was located at South Marston, a small village north-east of the main town. For much of its life the company had been responsible for aircraft manufacture. During the late1930s and war years, its workers designed and produced over 1000 South Marston Masters, RAF fighter pilot trainer aircraft that could match the speeds of Spitfires and Hurricanes. In 1940 it began manufacture of the Short Stirling bomber, eventually producing 16 per month. Later in the war it manufactured 121 Mk 21 Spitfires, one of which remained at the plant when I arrived there, greeting workers and visitors at the main gate. During the 1950s, the plant became the Supermarine Division of Vickers Armstrongs, primarily producing components and assemblies for the shipbuilding divisions but also diversifying into commercial electronics and other sectors.[1]

I spent my first year at the plant based in the apprentice training school, a large workshop equipped with milling machines, centre lathes, bench drills, grinders, fitters' benches, welding machinery and an electronics work room. Around 50 new apprentices were divided into teams of five, each of which progressed sequentially through the different skill areas until, towards the end of the year, individuals made a decision on which skill to specialise in. Although I shone on the centre lathes—one piece of work won an apprentice prize for its accuracy—I decided to base myself in electronics because I seemed to do well at fiddling around with various electronic components and circuits. I was joined by three other team members, Derek Prout, Ray Sheppard and Sam Cook. We became good friends. I was also friendly with a young Irish apprentice, Bernard. He had come over from the Falls Road area of Belfast and was living in digs locally. His parents would send him regular updates of the situation in their community and towards the end of the first year he came to me in a highly agitated state explaining that 'prods' had fired bullets through his parents' front door and he was going to Belfast to fight back. He departed a week later and he left me in little doubt that he was planning to join the IRA.

It was at the end of the first year that life became really interesting as we progressed from the training school to the factory shop floor. My little electronics team was posted to a large workshop holding around 100 workers responsible for the production of electronic blood dialysis machines. Little did I realise it at the time, but this section of the plant was a working example of the principle of arms conversion that would become a central feature of my trade union activism decades later. The workforce comprised teams of fitters, electricians and technicians who together would assemble, wire and test the machines. Derek, Ray, Sam and I were given instruction into how to wire sub-assemblies and final assembly machines from wiring diagrams. For novice apprentices this

---

[1] http://www.swindonweb.com/index.asp?m=8&s=116&ss=402 Swindon History, Planes, Trains and Automobiles, accessed 3 November 2020.

was interesting work at first, though as time bred familiarity with the various tasks it became clear that the work would eventually become fairly monotonous.

Monotony or not, it was the friendships and humour on the shop floor that I remember most fondly. Arriving more or less straight from school, I was fascinated by this. I had always been a fairly shy person outside of close circles of friends but I became drawn into a culture of working-class camaraderie. This was characterised by banter, swearing and jokes, the tricks played on workmates, tales of domestic lives, discussions of politics, TV, football, with the pitfalls of supporting Swindon Town and the sharing of life stories involving drunken nights, hangovers, women and sex, marital misbehaviour and so on.

Many workers had their own nicknames of which sadly I can remember only a few. There was Sexy Arthur, a man in his early sixties who in looks resembled Charles Hawtrey, the effete actor in the Carry On films, and who talked endlessly of the romances he could never have. Another was Bobby Bear, as the name suggests, a big, lovable, hirsute man who would regularly tease his mates. And there was Sleepy Ron. Nobody knew what he got up to at night but he was always falling asleep during the day. Perhaps he was moonlighting. One incident I do remember was when Sleepy Ron crawled into one of the main dialysis machine assemblies, structures shaped like coffins. Soon enough the sound of snoring came from within. Along came Bobby Bear who decided to sit on one of the port holes of this structure and relieve himself of some wind. The commotion that followed was talked about for days, indeed weeks afterwards. I also recall a lovely man named Alan Selman. He was a wheelchair user with a severe disability. A very talented mimic, he would regularly entertain colleagues with his impersonations of politicians, TV celebrities and sports people such as Brian Clough. His favourite was of the plummy-voiced BBC show jumping commentator Raymond Brooks-Ward who covered the 1971 Hickstead event. This was won by the Yorkshire-born working-class rider Harvey Smith who, in his lap of victory, proceeded to put two fingers up at the judges after an argument. Alan always ended this impersonation with the two fingers and a loud raspberry.

Occasionally I would witness examples of sexism at work, though as a young adult in my late teens I did not understand this as such, thinking that this was normal shop-floor behaviour. Some typical examples I recall include the case of the young blonde administrator, no older than me, who was based upstairs in a large fitting and machine shop adjacent to my workshop. Every time she completed the long walk through the shop, she had to endure a continual chorus of wolf-whistles from the men. Another was the woman in a workshop, probably in her forties, who was described by the men pejoratively as the 'company bike'. At the time workmates used to whisper that she was having an affair with a technician named Wheel who then became known, less pejoratively, as the 'Wheel of Fortune'.

I had no great interest in party politics in those early years. As an 18-year-old I voted for the first time in the 1970 general election for Harold Wilson's Labour, principally because my parents were lifelong supporters who had voted Labour in every general and local election since 1945. Also, my electrical supervisor in the training school urged us all to vote Labour as 'the party of the working man'. In a surprise result Ted Heath's Conservatives won. This proved to be the first election of many where my vote went to the losing party. I did gradually develop an interest in workplace politics, however. At the age of eighteen I joined a trade union, the EETPU. This was a new union formed from the 1968 merger of the Electrical Trades Union and The Plumbing Trades Union to become the Electrical, Electronic, Telecommunications and Plumbing Union. Its first General Secretary was Frank Chapple who became a hate figure of the left for his attacks on left activists in the union and on left-wing politics in general. Chapple was originally a Communist Party member who had left in 1956, partly as a result of the Soviet invasion of Hungary. It was the Electrical Trades Union ballot-rigging scandal of 1961—which helped the communist Frank Haxell to win the General Secretary election until overturned by the High Court—that provided the impetus for Chapple's drive against officials who were Communist Party members. Rule changes forced all such officials from full-time paid positions, though for a good number of years Party members remained as workplace stewards. At the Vickers plant the EETPU convenor, or senior steward, was another communist, Ted Poole. As a young apprentice I had no occasion to speak with him at work though a few years later that changed when I began an interest in folk music.

Ignoring the rhetoric of Frank Chapple and others, the workers I mixed with at Vickers had nothing but praise for Ted Poole. He was regarded as a man whose prime aim was to defend the interests of his members against arbitrary management. One of his close friends was a young man named Eric Stott who was the EETPU shop steward for the blood dialysis plant. It was Eric who persuaded me to join on the apprentice rate. He became a good friend in more ways than one. He certainly won me over to the benefits of trade unionism and the advantages of collectivism over fending for yourself. But he also politicised me in another way.

At that stage in my life I had kept alive my love of soul music. Before joining Vickers I had formed a soul band called Inert Blue with some school friends, and we won over local music fans with our exuberant energy more than our musical talent. I was the lead singer, strutting around in a mohair suit with a microphone in my hand, Otis Redding fashion. I had also lived my late teenage years as a 'mod', thus joining a sub-culture centred on fashion—the wearing of suits and smart shoes at night for visits to discos and parkas by day, riding scooters and hanging out at coffee houses. I had a Lambretta scooter, a parka covered in various homemade soul music insignia (for example, 'I love Sam and Dave') and I wore a single, precious mohair suit with my hair back-combed, Small Faces style. My local group of mod friends, mostly from Commonweal School and the Vickers training school, hung out in the evening at a small coffee house at the top of the hill on Victoria Street, drinking Coca Cola and playing soul and Tamla Motown music on an impressively stocked jukebox. We rarely missed the top black British soul bands that came to Swindon to play at the Locarno and the White Tiles disco, the likes of Geno Washington and the Ram Jam Band and my favourites, Ruby James and the Stax. We would dance the night away until closing time. The event I remember most vividly was travelling to Bristol's Colston Hall to see the touring Stax/Volt Revue concert. Most of the major Stax stars were on the bill, including Otis Redding, Sam and Dave, Eddie Floyd, Arthur Conley, Booker T and the MGs and the Mar-Keys. Thinking about it now, this was certainly the first, and I'm sure the only, gig I have been to where the audience comprised mostly black people.

The other competing subculture of the time was the 'rockers' or 'greasers' as we sometimes called them. Here, working-class lads rode powerful motorcycles and dressed in leather gear and jeans. At the height of the competition between the groups, organised fights broke out, typically on bank holidays at major south and east coast seaside resorts such as Margate, Clacton and Bournemouth. There were some incidents of this at Weston-super-Mare but thankfully my group of friends did not get involved. I eventually gave up the mod lifestyle for two reasons. First, as a movement it was on the wane by the end of the 1960s. Fashions were changing and my friends were already dabbling in becoming hippies. Also in Swindon, the lead mod, a young man named Des Rideout, who we all looked up to, was killed in a scooter accident in 1969. At the funeral, I along with another 100 or so of Swindon's scooter riders gave him a guard of honour. For me, it signified the end of a cultural moment. And in any case, I was learning to drive and would soon be purchasing an old Ford Popular 100E.

What has this got to do with my shop steward Eric Stott? Well, I was on the lookout for something new and he introduced me to something old that I hadn't encountered before, namely the protest folk music of Bob Dylan. I had of course encountered Bob Dylan in the mid-1960s. A friend of mine, Ken Brown, was a big fan of Dylan's folk rock material, and I used to play his *Highway 61 Revisited* and *Blonde on Blonde* albums a good deal round at his house. But the early folk music was absent. Eric lent me two albums, *The Freewheelin' Bob Dylan* and *The Times They Are A-Changin'*. I became transfixed by this music, especially the anti-war and civil rights protest songs, such as *With God on Our Side* and *The Lonesome Death of Hattie Carroll*. They caused me to begin to think about injustice and powerlessness in ways that national politicians had not. And it didn't end there. Eric also played guitar himself and could cover a good number of Dylan songs. To cut a long story short, he persuaded me to try to learn to play and gave me a cheap old instrument to try out. I spent around six months learning chords and tentatively trying to fingerpick. This was on a conventional right-handed guitar, whereas I am left-handed, and to this day I regret not learning on a left-handed instrument, in which case my playing might be much improved (as would my current banjo work). But this is to quibble. Eric introduced me to exciting new music and the possibility of playing a musical instrument for the first time, and I was hooked.

I began walking around to his parents' house on the Park council estate not far from where I lived and playing duets of Dylan, Woody Guthrie, Pete Seeger and others in his bedroom. To improve things, I eventually splashed out on a £25 Yamaha jumbo acoustic (right-handed). Eric would also play me music from his large album collection, introducing me to the blues of Robert Johnson, Son House, Charlie Patton, Blind Lemon Jefferson and others. Miraculously, the great Son House played a gig at the Swindon Town Hall, I think in late 1970. Son

House was helped on to the stage, played half a dozen of his classics (most memorably *Death Letter Blues*), completely stunned the audience and was then helped off. He died a few years later.

During the early 1970s, my playing improved and I even wrote my first song, a protest song, *The Ballad of Samuel Devenney*, about a man who was beaten up and killed by RUC officers in Londonderry in 1969 and regarded as the first victim of the Troubles. Sadly, those were the days of pen and paper and I no longer have the lyrics. At some point in 1972 Eric persuaded me to come to the Swindon folk club to play it. In those days there existed a close affinity between British folk clubs and Communist Party activism, as the genre's focus on working class history and oppression sat well with left-wing politics. The Swindon club was run by Ted Poole, my communist EETPU convenor. I arrived with my guitar and very nervously—and badly—played the song along with a more traditional blues number, *Rocks and Gravel*. Despite this the *Ballad of Samuel Devenney* went down well and Ted Poole was kind to me that night and gave me much encouragement.

I realise I have embarked upon a brief musical digression here and I need to get back to the workplace. In any case, my flirtation with musical stardom came to an end a few years later when I got married and had kids. I didn't pick up an instrument to play seriously again until nearly 40 years later.

I have few other recollections of working at Vickers. I did spend a period of time as a lone apprentice in a small hydraulics design workshop comprising four slightly eccentric graduate engineers. The engineers would give me electronic wiring diagrams and I would create strange three-dimensional circuits using an array of resistors, diodes, transistors and capacitors. When completed they resembled small modern sculptural creations and, apparently, they worked when a voltage source was connected to their input leads. The strangest thing that happened, and it made the main evening news that day, was when one of the engineers was arrested and detained for hoarding war-time guns in his attic. Presumably the police were tipped off when he was seen giving a few of them an airing in his garden. The collection included a World War Two Vickers machine gun.

I probably spent around six months in the workshop. During this time, I had the happy experience of benefitting from the repercussions of the 1972 miners' strike, a dispute over pay. This began on the 9th January 1972 and lasted until the day after my twentieth birthday,

28th February. For decades, miners' wages had fallen behind those of comparable industrial workers and the National Union of Mineworkers, despite a number of local disputes over the years, had failed to use its muscle to correct this. As the dispute wore on, the Central Electricity Generating Board began cutting power to homes and businesses and I was sent home by Vickers management on full pay (around £6 per week) on a number of occasions. I and my fellow apprentices began to realise that trade unionism can truly be a force for good! And I surely noted that the miners eventually won a 20% pay rise.

My only other achievement at the plant was when I managed to read all three volumes of Tolkien's *Lord of The Rings* during a two-week stint in a radiography darkroom. Sent there during the factory's summer holiday shutdown—I had permission to take my holiday outside of the shutdown and the darkroom worked continuously throughout the year—my job was to lift X-ray films of metal structures from one developer/fixer tank to the next whenever an alarm bell sounded. Typically, this was every 10 minutes. I could spend most of the working day with my book propped up underneath a red darkroom light. This did little for the strength of my eyesight; neither did the three books do much for my literary enjoyment. But the X-ray shift did allow me to go on a continental holiday with four of my school friends. We clubbed together to buy a clapped-out Bedford Dormobile that we were confident could make a 3000-mile trip. The rear section was converted to allow all five of us to sleep there if required, though we also carried a frame tent. Our trip took us though the length of France to the Riviera, then west to Northern Italy, north through the Italian and Swiss Alps, then briefly to western Germany, then Paris and finally Cherbourg. Apart from the scenery, what stays in the memory mostly involved the intake of alcohol. On the way from Saint Tropez to Nice we stayed at a small coastal resort, Juan-les-Pins, and found a quiet bar where we occupied a table for the evening. There we consumed glass after glass of a drink that was foreign to our inchoate tastes, Pernod. We managed to consume so much of it because it was cheap and very easy to drink, with no apparent side effects. Until we all stood up to go that is, when simultaneously we fell over, incapable of little apart from crawling to our van and managing a hot and sweaty sleep with hangovers all round in the morning. On another occasion, when walking a tortuous road that wound its way up to the streets of Monaco sitting atop a cliff, one of our number, Norman, with perhaps a beer too many under his belt, decided to take the direct route and attempted to climb the cliff itself. He was spotted by a police car, arrested and then spent much of the night in a police cell.

While walking the length of the Saint Tropez harbourside I was shocked by the extent and size of wealth on display. We passed huge privately owned pleasure boats and sailing ships large enough to carry multiple households and carrying luxuries such as private helicopters and the like. That day, I fell out with some of my friends who could see nothing wrong with flaunting such wealth whereas I argued it was a case for communism.

As we approached Paris on our journey home, our standard three gear Dormobile lost top gear so we had to complete the remainder of the journey in first and second, a long and slow trip. Staying in a small village just south of Paris the night before Bastille Day we managed to gatecrash a Bastille party in the village hall. We were made to feel very welcome and I can remember having the time of my life drinking cider, red wine, surviving this and dancing to live music with the local girls all night long.

A development in the summer of 1972 was to catalyse a major change in my working life and bring the time I had enjoyed at the Vickers plant to an end. All UK engineering apprentices took day release at local technical colleges to study either City and Guilds courses, if a craft apprentice, or the Ordinary and Higher National Certificate (ONC/HNC) if a technician apprentice. I was one of the latter and although I did well in the mathematics and engineering drawing modules, I never truly grasped electrical engineering science. Despite this I somehow achieved an overall merit in the ONC final exams. As a result, a few weeks into July, I was called in by my apprentice training manager to discuss the idea of my studying for a BSc in Electronics at Bath University, sponsored by the company. He urged me to take up this offer. I was not so sure but after discussion with my parents I decided it was seen to be the right thing to do, even though my inner self was sounding alarm bells. When I returned to my pals in the blood dialysis plant and told them the news, they all wished me well but I was decidedly circumspect and very reluctant to leave behind the factory life.

1973: Bath University and Coventry

The university accepted the company's application on my behalf and, in September, I made my way to the campus to register, driving by then an old beaten-up Austin Mini. On the way I was nearly killed. In those days the A46 into Bath travelled steeply downhill towards a set of traffic lights where a right turn took vehicles into the city. There was a bit of a traffic queue at these lights as I waited patiently on the hill. Suddenly, unbeknown to me, a large heavily laden lorry came down the hill, lost its brakes and careered into the traffic behind me creating a concertina pile-up. My mini crashed into another lorry in front carrying steel girders and part of its metal frame crashed through my windscreen stopping literally an inch in front of my face. I was not badly injured but obviously severely shaken. The police at the incident told me I was extremely lucky to be alive. Not an auspicious start.

As a first-year student I did not have the conventional experience of meeting sizeable numbers of new students in accommodation blocks or flats. I was a late applicant, and someone who owned a car, and was therefore placed in farmhouse accommodation at Norton St Philip, a village some miles south of Bath. Upon arrival, I was greeted by a friendly and rather posh landlady who introduced me to three other current students, all second and third years. There were two more guys who had dropped out in the previous year and were now working locally. It was a strange set up, more like holiday bed and breakfast accommodation. We didn't have to shop or cook our own meals as, at the ring of a bell, we all arrived at the dining room where the landlady provided large, cooked breakfasts each morning and three-course meals in the evening. I didn't really fit in there and I lost out on the potential friendships and nightlife of Bath. I certainly missed Vickers. Worse still, my room-mate was a drippy evangelical Christian who spent his time pining for his girlfriend or weeping over the film *Love Story* which he had seen well over 50 times. And then there was the course. I could not engage with this at all and it merely proved that I never would have a grasp of the principles of electrical engineering science as my ONC study had already suggested. At the end of the Easter term in 1973 I sat down and had a discussion with my course tutor and by mutual consent I decided to leave.

I did not tell my parents until the summer term and in the meantime tried some local temporary work. This also meant I would join the dropouts at the farmhouse who were now close to outnumbering the students. The first job I took on was at the local chicken processing plant in the village. I have to say the outcome was not favourable. I walked off the job after just four hours. The plant's layout was a paragon of simplicity: essentially a long rectangular building where lorries offloaded crates of horrifically overcrowded chickens at one end and packaged frozen chicken emerged at the other. Inside the building a labour-intensive operation murdered the chickens (I did not venture down that end), plucked them, removed heads, necks and giblets and placed the remaining bodies on assembly line hooks which allowed operatives further down the line to clean up the innards and outer appearance of each bird before packaging and freezing. My job was to stand on the line and, as each bird approached, I would hold a still warm body in the palm of one hand and with the other insert a suction pipe to remove unwanted material which it did with a noisy slurping sound. I wore factory overalls which soon became blood spattered, though the worst of it was the smell of chicken flesh. I was mightily relieved when the lunch horn sounded. I removed my overalls and walked out, never to return. I rarely ate chicken again and, a decade later with Eileen's prompting—I have yet to introduce her—became a vegetarian.

I then became employed at the Watney-Ushers brewery in Trowbridge. My position was on the cask production line doing little more than lifting empty casks, which were still pretty heavy, from one belt to the next. I had to be on the lookout for various health and safety risks, but the greatest came from the man stood next to me, who suffered from diabetes. Whether it was the constant aroma of beer in the atmosphere or the free beer workers enjoyed during each shift I do not know, but on occasion each day he would clearly suffer from hyperglycaemia, become very angry and hurl a casket through the air. I moved on from the brewery after around a month. Years later I read an article in a *CAMRA* newspaper and discovered that the plant was closed in 2000 and sold to Kim-Jong Il of North Korea. Websites give reports of tour organisers explaining that, according to North Korean folklore, the women of Trowbridge forced the brewery to close in protest at the men coming home drunk each day. There may be an element of truth in this.[2]

By the time I left, Swindon Borough Council had sent a letter to my parents explaining that I was no longer in receipt of a student grant and would have to pay back a term's portion. The cat was out of the bag. They were of course annoyed, but not as angry as I feared. In any case, I had already decided not to return home because, coincidentally, a large part of the Vickers Armstrongs plant was closing down as part

---

2 https://boakandbailey.com/2020/05/ushers-of-trowbridge-brewery-history Usher's of Trowbridge: disappearing one brick at a time, accessed 5 November 2020.

of a companywide rationalisation that would become all too common elsewhere in the years to come. The training school management offered me the chance to complete a final year of my apprenticeship but I decided that with three years of training under my belt plus an ONC I could find employment in engineering elsewhere. A close school friend, Ken Brown, had moved to Coventry and I opted to join him.

The move to Coventry proved to be another life changing event, though this was not apparent at first. GEC was one of the city's largest employers and I targeted it immediately. In May 1973, I was interviewed but although formally successful the managers had indicated from the beginning that they could offer no immediate employment and I would have to join a waiting list. So, biding my time, I went in search of a short-term alternative and landed at Skyline Electronics where I was employed fixing TV aerials to the city's houses and high-rise flats. This was not really my cup of tea, though I survived for a few months. I worked with a teammate named Leroy whose parents were Jamaican immigrants. Leroy was a very popular member of the small workforce and his managers and other Skyline workers affectionately called him 'Sooty'. It was 1973, a time when such language was mainstream on TV comedy shows and the like. Affectionate or not I knew it was racist but challenging it as a newly arrived young upstart required a level of courage that I did not possess. I would almost certainly have been ostracised or worse. Leroy told me it didn't bother him, or so he said.

What did bother Leroy was my antics with ladders. I had to carry heavy three-section industrial ladders from our van to each building, extend them to the house gutters and then climb the ladder with one hand clutching an extra-heavy roof ladder which I would then attach to the roof once I had made it to the top. When I had climbed up to the chimney stack, I felt safe but it was the getting there and coming back down that I had difficulty with. If any passer-by had carried a movie camera, they would have captured some good film of a Stan Laurel character swinging and swaying dangerously on various ladders and roofs. By mutual consent I decided to move on after a couple of months.

I then found a job at another local electronics firm repairing faulty jukeboxes and gambling machines in Coventry's public houses and clubs. Had the repair work taken place in a workshop I might well have been content with this for a time. But it didn't. All repairs were conducted in situ under the gaze of the pub customers and this regularly caused me some anxiety. In those days the jukebox provided the only source of music in the big city-centre pubs and young punters enjoyed the hits of the day playing in the background while they were knocking back beers and shorts on their way to nightclubs. Much as they do today. What they didn't like was when the music stopped. In those days many of Coventry's pubs were large industrial affairs providing alcohol to the city's engineering and car workers. Whenever I was called out to repair a machine I would hope and pray that the problem was merely a 45-rpm record that had slipped and caused a jam in its stack or on the carrier arm. That was two minutes work to fix. But just as likely was a more serious problem that required electrical components or wiring to be replaced. I might take an hour or more over this, or worse still, take the machine away. On such occasions I would regularly have to suffer the quips and cat calls from the punters: "Call yourself an engineer you twat", that type of thing. The one perk of the job, however, was that the company gave me a minivan both for work and private use and I suspect this kept me employed at the company for longer than I had anticipated.

Nevertheless, by the winter of 1973 I had virtually given up on GEC and began to make plans to search for work in Bristol where the British Aircraft Corporation (BAC) was regularly advertising very large numbers of vacancies. This was with some reluctance because I did enjoy aspects of the Coventry social life. I lived in a flat with Ken Brown, just a five-minute walk from Highfield Road, then the home of Coventry City football club. They were a top-quality Division One team in those days and we would regularly go to matches to watch some of the top teams, especially my old club from my London youth, West Ham. We also spent many evenings, work permitting, in the pubs and clubs. Ken Brown had a girlfriend, a Coventry and Warwick trainee nurse named Eileen McNicholas. She, her best friend Eileen Lake, another trainee nurse, and her boyfriend would sometimes come with us.

The first time I set eyes upon Eileen Lake was when I woke up from deep slumber on a bench seat in the Mr George nightclub at around 2.00am. I have never been able to hold large quantities of beer and my sleep episodes were not unusual. With hair down to my shoulders and a generally dishevelled look she can't have been very impressed. Nevertheless, she must have seen some slight glimmer of potential because within two months we would be together.

1974-1979: British Aircraft Corporation and BICC

1974-77: Life on the shop floor

In January 1974 I travelled to BAC Guided Weapons (GW) Division in Bristol to attend an interview, having applied just before Christmas. The plant shared an airfield site at Filton with its sister division, BAC Commercial Aircraft Division. At that time, they together employed over 10,000 workers. On the other side of the A38 that ran past the two plants was a large Rolls Royce Military Aircraft site which itself employed 10,000 workers; this was a huge aerospace complex employing around 20,000 workers, albeit a decline from over 30,000 employed in the 1950-60s. The GW plant was desperate for labour at the time I applied, having won large weapons contracts with the UK government. I had no moral scruples about working for such a company although I did in my later years as a union activist. I was not a pacifist, I assumed that the UK's armed services were necessary for the country's defence and that they required the necessary equipment to do this. I had no real consciousness of arms exports in those early days. Moreover, I came to realise that labour markets are structured partially by geography and the paths taken historically by large employers. In Bristol if you were a skilled engineering worker, or a prospective apprentice seeking employment, then you had little choice but to enter the industry. And the work was indeed generally highly skilled, and at times challenging, compared to mass production industries. It was also relatively well paid and secure.

In saying that, my interview was rudimentary to say the least. I had a ten-minute chat with a friendly supervisor who I discovered subsequently had previously been an EETPU shop steward. I was asked to identify certain electronic components and then offered a job as a quality control inspector with an immediate start. By that time, I had left the jukebox repair firm so I accepted the offer. Ironically within days of this I received a letter from GEC at Coventry offering me a position but it was too late, my mind was made up.

I found somewhere to stay temporarily. An old school friend was living in a house at Pucklechurch, just a few miles from Filton, and he put me up until I had found a place to live in the city. Later in January, back in Coventry, my friend Ken Brown held a leaving party for both of us since he planned a move back to Swindon. I can't remember much about the party itself but as was my habit I eventually fell asleep on the sofa in the flat's lounge and woke up in the morning to find Eileen Lake asleep next to me. This was the start of a romance that continues to this day. We commenced seeing each other as regularly as we could, when I would drive up to Coventry at weekends in another beaten up old Mini to stay at her shared rented house.

My job title at BAC was Electronics Quality Control Inspector. I had really wanted a job as a technician in the Electronics Test Department but my humble experience of testing and repairing, or not repairing, public house juke boxes was deemed insufficient. At that time the sister division, BAC Commercial Aircraft, outsourced much of its electronics work to the BAC GW Filton site. For my first year I found myself assigned to some of this work, checking printed circuit board assemblies manufactured for the air intake control system of the supersonic aircraft Concorde which was manufactured at Filton. I worked harmoniously with a small team of inspectors. As the youngest member of the team and known to be a bit of a daydreamer I was often the butt of my colleagues' jokes, but this didn't bother me. The basic printed circuit boards were complex affairs comprising multiple circuits (or tracks) sandwiched between laminate boards. They were manufactured at the GW Filton site by a large unit that specialised in producing commercial boards, probably one of the earliest successful examples of defence diversification at BAC. Once complete, shop floor operators assembled an array of integrated circuits to each board and my job was to check these against electronic wiring diagrams.

As soon as I started work at the plant, I contacted my EETPU senior steward to renew my membership. During my time at Bath University and the short spell in Coventry I had lost touch with the union. I did not resign since I was unaware of the need to do so. Equally, I had paid no union subscriptions for some time because, even when employed, the companies concerned were small and not unionised. My steward advised me that, as I was already a member, he could begin collecting subs on the spot. Around one month later I was surprised to receive a letter from the EETPU Regional Secretary asking me to attend a disciplinary hearing for non-payment of subs over the previous year. This was itemised on the agenda for a union branch meeting at the Stag and Hounds, Old Market, Bristol. The steward told me not to worry about this and that I would receive a small fine measured in pence. With some trepidation I climbed the stairs to the packed upstairs hall. I sat at the back and watched proceedings, my first union meeting. When they came to the disciplinary item my name was eventually called and I had to walk to the front of the hall to face the officers at the main table. Asked why I had paid no subscriptions for well over a year I responded with a red face, nervously blurting out that I was innocent, that I had no way of paying subs in my situation. Following a few whispers across the table they fined me £4, around a fifth of my weekly wage! Needless to say, this was not the most auspicious introduction to the more mundane mechanics of local union activity.

During my first couple of months at BAC I had my second experience of the repercussions of a national miners' strike. The early 1970s were marked by high levels of global inflation, caused partly by fast-rising oil prices exacerbated by the 1973 Yom Kippur War. To tackle this, Ted Heath's Conservative government introduced a cap on public sector pay rises and by persuasion attempted to place limits on private sector wage settlements. By the middle of 1973, Britain's miners found their wages deteriorating markedly, below the level recommended by the Wilberforce Inquiry. In November 1973, the NUM rejected a National Coal Board pay offer and implemented an overtime ban. Coal stocks began to deplete and by the end of December Ted Heath announced a national three-day week to conserve stocks by reducing electricity consumption. The miners responded on 24th January by rejecting a 16.5% pay rise and voting overwhelmingly for an all-out strike. Ted Heath then called a general election which resulted in him losing his overall majority. A minority Labour government came to power in March 1974 and immediately settled, offering the miners a 35% increase. So my apprenticeship in studying the efficacy of collective trade union strength continued during this period when my initial employment at BAC was reduced to two days a week. I cannot remember complaining about this.

When life got back to normal my section was offered plentiful overtime and occasional night shifts as management attempted to reduce the backlog caused by the weekly closures. I did complete one stint of nights. My inspection team and the shop floor operators were able to manage any daytime sleep disorder by unlocking the foremen's offices each night and taking it in turns to have a few hours' sleep. We were never caught, night-time supervision being almost completely absent. Had such newspapers as the Daily Mail or the local Bristol Evening Post got hold of our story, no doubt we would have been exposed as yet more examples of 'lazy British workers' at the 'BAC holiday camp' as it was known locally. By contrast, we just felt that continual swapping between day and night shifts can damage your health, you just didn't feel quite right, and we had no scruples in taking the chance to mitigate the effects.

In the spring Eileen moved to Bristol to take up employment as a trainee general nurse at the Bristol Royal Infirmary. Initially her accommodation was at the former Dr Fox's psychiatric hospital at Brislington, a grim Victorian building said to be haunted, which had been converted into nurses' accommodation. I was not allowed into the building. Before long though she had found a bed-sit in Chandos Road, Redland and I was living nearby in another bed-sit in Cranbrook Road, a ten-minute walk away. Although we often stayed at each other's bedsit we did not consider living together initially, though that would change within a year or so.

The remainder of 1974 was uneventful, working by day or night and spending as much time as I could with Eileen, either hanging out at each other's flats or going to pubs or nightclubs, such as Vadims in Clifton, to dance, with occasional cinema visits to see such Hollywood favourites as *Chinatown* and *Mean Streets*.

In early 1975 I was transferred to an inspection team in the GW plant's main electronics manufacturing centre, the Product Support Group (PSG). This housed around 40 inspectors and nearly 200 electronics operators, including a good number of women, divided between the manufacture of guidance simulators and power unit assemblies for the Swingfire and Rapier guided weapons systems. Also present were teams of foremen, rate fixers and production managers, along with inspection foremen and a chief inspector, John Morris, who did little else most days but walk around the plant scowling at people.

The basic labour process comprised constructing a large three-dimensional metal frame that would eventually fit into metal boxes the size of a suitcase; assembled to the frame would be printed circuit board assemblies and an array of electronic and electro-mechanical components, such as relays and transformers. The operators wired the components together in accordance with different wiring diagrams, creating fairly complex wiring looms in the process. The inspectors would then check that the right components had been fitted and that they were adequately soldered and correctly wired using a battery-operated wire tracer. A typical unit such as a simulator took three or four days to inspect. Completing one job generated some job satisfaction;

working on the same assembly type carrying out the same routines week after week generated tedium. Invariably faults would be found in the operators' work and these were sent back for correction. This could at times cause a major argument with the less able operators, since the time spent on correcting a considerable quantity of faults affected the shop bonus system, which I shall later come to. In one of the worst confrontations an operator, who was notorious for his evil temper, threw a complete simulator assembly at me. Luckily this caused only bruises to my shoulder. Fortunately for him this was not witnessed by any of the production foremen, and I was not the kind of person to report him.

We all enjoyed a good deal of camaraderie on the shopfloor. Although we were separated by job function into operators and inspectors—and the fact that we constituted different union bargaining groups could occasionally cause tensions and rivalries—we worked side by side and mixed socially. I developed many friendships with the operators, people like Nigel Redman, Chris Isaacs, John Buckle, Dave Oakley and the union convenor, Frank Tamlyn, friendships that have in some cases lasted to this day. The camaraderie was cemented by the strength of the EETPU on the ground. Both EETPU sections (operators and inspectors) ran a closed shop, and both, though especially the operators, were prepared to threaten or take different forms of industrial action to defend member interests. Everyone recognised the strength of the union and it provided a strong sense of security and confidence that allowed us to work at our own pace, to stop and chat when we felt like it and to lark about on occasion without fear of management retribution. Some may call this union supported laziness, I call it the ability to enjoy a satisfactory quality of working life.

My friend, Frank Tamlyn, the EETPU convenor at the Guided Weapons Filton plant recalled how he had little difficulty in mobilising his members during the 1970s. As he put it,

> the bottom line was that the company knew I could take two hundred people out of the plant, they knew that and you've seen it happen. I could take them out and they [the members] wouldn't even ask why they're going out.[3]

This should not be taken to imply that the plant was subject to regular all out strikes in this period, because that was not the case. However,

3 Interview with Frank Tamlyn, November 2003

smaller scale, though highly effective, official and unofficial actions were common. Disputes over pay disparity, bonus payments, member grievances and disciplinary issues were often settled to the union's advantage following actions such as half-day stoppages, overtime bans, walking out on to the main A38 road that ran by the plant and stopping traffic for an hour or two, or most commonly of all, dropping tools and occupying another production area or a department in the office areas to bring work to a halt. A popular course of action was to invade the Personnel Department and take over the offices of the various personnel managers. Another was to occupy the company board room located in Filton House by the main gate on the A38. Frank Tamlyn remembered a further example that stirred up a good deal of managerial animosity:

> The worst one for the company was when we took over the management mess, they took that very personal. That's around the back of the canteen, we went in there and they all came over for their lunch and we were all sat in there. They didn't like that. In fact, they seemed to react more to that particular takeover than any of the others.

The vast majority of these disputes and actions at that time were between management and the EETPU, AUEW and TGWU shop floor operators' unions. However, the first industrial action that I was involved with, almost as soon as I joined the PSG unit, involved primarily the EETPU inspectors' section and the two white collar unions: AUEW-TASS which represented technical workers and APEX which represented clerical workers. The 1970s was the decade of the advent of defined benefit occupational pension schemes. The BAC dispute concerned the company's proposal to dismantle the existing miserly staff pension scheme to which members contributed a very small amount each month, literally pence, and received an equally small pension in return. The new pension proposal required members to contribute a larger percentage of their wages and the company would add its own contribution. The disagreement was partly over the level of respective contributions but primarily about workers' rights of representation on the pension committees and board of trustees. If we were being asked to contribute a greater proportion of our wages then, in return, we demanded some control over pension benefits. When negotiations failed to make sufficient headway, the inspectors and technical staff took joint action to put pressure on the company. On one occasion, following a mass meeting, we mounted a picket on the entrance to our PSG building and all operators then immediately stopped work. On another day we did the same at the entrance of the plant's main drawing office and brought all work to a halt. A feature of these internal occupations was that all security staff who controlled entrance to many of the main buildings were members of the TGWU and immediately themselves stopped work when requested to allow the picketing or occupation to take place. AUEW-TASS members also took part in these actions and as a result of the disruption, the company came to an acceptable agreement: we were to contribute 6% of wages, the company contributed a further 9%, and staff representation on pension committees, which in effect meant union representation, was conceded. The new scheme was later applied to the manual workforce. This was one of the few occasions when the company's non-manual unions had taken the lead in a dispute to the subsequent benefit of the manual workers.

Unlike the following decade there were only occasional disputes over general pay increases. The main reason for this was that we were in the decade of pay restraint imposed by both Conservative and Labour governments. I do remember very clearly receiving monthly pay increases during 1974 and '75, which were a hangover from the previous government of Ted Heath. Stage Three of Heath's counter-inflation policy limited wage increases to £2.25 per week but with threshold safeguards if inflation rose above seven percent, which it did! This was eventually superseded by the voluntary wage restraint of the Social Contract imposed by the 1974-79 Labour government.

On the other hand, I witnessed many disputes, both collective and individual, involving unofficial industrial action mounted primarily by the EETPU operators and centred on the shop floor bonus system. The bonus was critical to an operator's weekly income, nearly 50% of the weekly wage. The system was similar to piecework principles.

Rate fixers would assess the time that should be taken to complete a job. Individual bonus payments were authorised every Wednesday, providing the prerequisite number of hours for the job, divided into weeks, were duly completed on time. If the target time was beaten, then more bonus would be paid. Payment of the bonus was generated by a job card—called a P10—which was fed into the wages system. Operators could save these up, if they so wished, so as to collect a larger bonus at a chosen time, at Christmas for example.

Management's problem was that, unlike the short times associated with piecework systems, the duration of operators' wiring jobs could vary between a few hours and five or six weeks. Establishing precise times for each job using time and motion study techniques was not feasible. Instead, the system relied upon rate fixers assessing the work remotely and setting a target. If any operator disagreed in advance, then the shop steward was called in and the work put into dispute. In such cases, which were very common, the operator was paid shop average bonus. The secret for the operators was then to ensure that the shop average kept increasing.

The challenge for Frank Tamlyn and his stewards was to minimise the incidence of poor performance, since this dragged the average bonus down. On the other hand, when operators beat the target times, they would gain financially and so would the shop because the average bonus paid then went up. Individual stewards had also to guard against rogue operators beating their targets too excessively. This ran the risk of rate fixers re-assessing target times. My inspector's bench was located right outside the door of the rate fixers office and I lost count of the number of times I witnessed arguments and rows which on occasion could culminate in tears. Most shopfloor operators regarded the rate fixers as obnoxious people. They used to call them "rat catchers".

They were all hard men but Frank generally had the beating of them. He often said to me that negotiating the payment of a shop average bonus was one of his greatest achievements because in a way the operators just could not lose. If their times beat the rate fixer's target they gained. If there was disagreement over the target or it could not be met, then members would call in their shop steward and if not resolved they received the shop average which they were invariably satisfied with. And Frank was well skilled in playing managers off against each other. He decided it was to his advantage to build up a close working relationship with the chief rate fixer, Martin Roberts, who was located elsewhere in the plant. If he emerged from a bruising encounter with one of the four PSG fixers, he would walk over to Martin Roberts' office. Roberts—whose main objective at work, it seems, was to have a quiet life— would say, "What's your problem Frank?" Invariably Frank would explain that the rate fixers were giving unfair times on the bonus forms (P10) and then Roberts would merely, in his unmistakeable black felt tip pen, write in the times that Frank requested. On this Frank said,

So whatever the fixers had done he [Martin Roberts] completely undermines straightaway. So I came back into PSG with all these P10s with great big fat black felt tip pens all over them. I mean the fixers hated it, they hated it. I mean their hands were tied, weren't they?

The bonus system could also be exploited for novel forms of industrial action. During the period of pay restraint, disputes over the relative worth of basic pay could be fought by manipulating the bonus. For example, on one occasion, Frank Tamlyn called a shop meeting and instructed all members to retain their P10s in their locked bench drawers if they were marked for less than the shop average. This meant that the shop average bonus payment could only go up. Of course, management eventually discovered this when they found that Frank had persuaded the timekeeper to let him into his office and prevent the missing P10s from being marked on operators' clock cards. The timekeeper got into trouble but the action was effective for a while.

Incidents of disciplinary action taken by management were common but the strength of the shop floor unions in virtually every case prevented outright sackings. If a member was threatened, a mass meeting followed by a half day walkout would invariably cause management to back down. As Frank Tamlyn put it,

But nobody got the sack if I didn't want them to in there. Nobody. We had some real horrendous ones, people I would have sacked let alone saved them.

But the unions did save them. One case I remember very well was of two operators, both popular on the shop floor, young and married with children, who had worked Sundays at double time for months. But more often than not they clocked out at 12.00 for lunch, went to the local pub a mere five minutes' walk from the site and stayed there until the late afternoon. Meanwhile an accomplice clocked them back in at 12.30. All of this was possible because the PSG foremen did not like coming in on Sundays. Eventually the foremen were tipped off, or they realised what was going on, and one Sunday afternoon they came in and waited for the two operators to return from the pub. The two were dismissed for gross misconduct. Their local shop steward at the time was Charlie Fenwick, who in later years I got to know very well. Charlie went behind the backs of the local foremen and production superintendent and went to plead with the site director responsible for production, Alf Gale. I think Charlie spun a good story about their young families and the dire effect of losing their jobs. The two operators were let off with a final warning. Another example was of an operator who was caught performing his Tarzan routine one evening, swinging from one end of the PSG building to the other on lamp holders high up in the ceiling of the building. I was amazed the first time I saw this. The foremen didn't even bother taking up a disciplinary case, knowing they would lose it.

I do not recall any formal disciplinary cases on my own inspection section in this period but there were two notable instances of shop steward theft of membership subscription payments. Each week stewards would collect subscriptions directly from their members and then hand the money to their chief steward, the union convenor, who paid the site total into the union account at a local bank. The system called 'check-off' was introduced later in 1979. This involved the company deducting subscriptions at source and transferring the total money collected to the union concerned. Most members preferred the traditional hand collections because it brought us into regular contact with our stewards, enabling discussions on company issues, politics, personal problems and so on. Early in 1976 we had a new local steward who looked after our section. I cannot remember his name, but he was a kindly sort though, strangely, he avoided discussing union matters with us in any depth. One day it came to light that he had not handed the subs to his convenor for three or four weeks and had instead, on his own admission, spent it on a new hi-fi system. It then emerged that he had completely hoodwinked his convenor because he was not even a union member! We of course were enraged, but he was not sacked—privately management must have been amused—and instead moved away elsewhere on site for his own protection. The second more serious case came later in the same year. A senior steward had clearly got into serious personal debt and the national union discovered that he had not paid in the site subs for a couple of months. This would have been a sizeable amount of money. When discovered he just left the company. I suppose the moral of this story is that whilst the system of steward collections was preferable in certain respects, it did have some flaws.

In the domestic sphere, Eileen and I were enjoying life as much as we could. I was working a fair amount of overtime, saving up for a deposit on a house. We both developed friendships with the electronics

With Eric Stott on my wedding day, 24th July 1976.

operators Nigel Redman, John Buckle and Chris Isaacs, along with their respective partners. We regularly had nights out in local Bristol pubs where Nigel and John introduced me to the pleasures of real ale. Nigel, Chris and I also shared the love of what we now call Americana, the likes of early Bruce Springsteen, John Prine and Loudon Wainwright. I also kept in touch with some of my old friends from Swindon, particularly Eric Stott and Ken Brown and, for five consecutive years, we spent weekends camping at the Cambridge Folk Festival to see performers such as John Prine, Steve Goodman, Loudon Wainwright, Arlo Guthrie, Bert Jansch, John Hartford, Ralph McTell and Don Mclean. Eileen came along to some of these and was a particular fan of Loudon Wainwright, who was always entertaining with his wry observations of everyday life in the USA.

Another pleasure was playing in Frank Tamlyn's pub skittles team. We were called Tam's People. The team had ten members, led by Frank the captain, and included Nigel, John, Chris, me and other shop-floor workers. We played regularly in a BAC league at different pub and social club venues. I really enjoyed those matches. Frank used to ham it up as captain with his team tactics, his words of advice and mad exuberance whenever we had managed to knock a few skittles down or better still, won the match. Team members played in pairs against opponent pairs and fairly often I was paired with Frank for the final round. Those final rounds could be marked by high drama as the result of the match often hinged on the final pair scores. As far as my own ability was concerned, I think I could be classed as a model of inconsistency. In some matches, when we depended on a high final score and all was silent as I took aim, my ball would go sailing down the alley to hit the kingpin at a perfect angle, sending many skittles flying, occasionally the lot. Then my whole team would erupt in celebration. Other times, the ball might slip out of my hand and fly into the air to land in the return gully. Ignominy.

The summer of 1976 was notable for two reasons. It was a drought year with days of blue skies and hot temperatures more or less continuously from March to September. It was also the year that Eileen and I got married. We had already moved in together at the beginning of the year, renting a small cottage in Stoke Bishop. We decided to tie the knot in the summer. On 24th July, another oppressively hot day, we were married at my parents' local catholic church in Amersham. Eileen was not catholic. I was brought up a catholic by my parents who were both supporters of liberation theology, it is true, but devout believers, nevertheless. I freed myself from the church at the age of 14 when my family moved to Swindon. Luckily for me, at that time there were no catholic secondary schools and so I drifted away, stopped going to church and, not wishing to cause my parents upset, I just did not discuss it with them. On the other hand, I knew they would be upset if we had decided to have a civil ceremony and, as this was a time when church weddings were still the norm, we both agreed to have a fairly small wedding in Amersham. Maybe, however, there was something stirring up in the heavens. The priest who took the ceremony was Dutch and he took it upon himself to give an unfathomable sermon of record length at a time in the afternoon when temperatures were reaching a peak. During this Eileen fainted at the altar and had to be carried out by me and my elder brother. My dad often recalled what happened and insisted that at this point my younger brother, Tony, who was playing the church organ, had hit the opening bars of Shostakovich's Funeral March.

We had a short five-day honeymoon in Paris, staying at a small hotel in the Pigalle, the city's old red-light district. Paris was even hotter and drier than Bristol and when we awoke on the first morning after a night of entertainment and too much alcohol we were parched. Due to city-wide water shortages, the hotel's supply of bottled water had run out. I

Eileen in Paris, July 1976.

remember walking tentatively around local streets with a hangover until I found some bottles of coca cola to bring back to Eileen. On another occasion we were walking down a small street heading back to our hotel. On one side was a prostitute screaming insults at a small man on the other side who was pulling faces at her. As we walked between them a glass bottle came flying through the air narrowly missing our heads.

During the mid-1970s I became a fan of Bristol City football club. I first went to a packed Ashton Gate in September 1975 to watch City play my old team West Ham in a league cup tie. City were a Division Two side then and lost 3-1 to West Ham, Clyde Best scoring twice for the Hammers. Following this I commenced going regularly with Nigel Redman and Chris Isaacs. 1975-76 was a good season for City, we were promoted to Division One for the first time. The club managed to stay in the top division for four years with such notable players as Tom Ritchie, Paul Cheesley, Clive Whitehead and Gerry Gow. Once established we signed some big names who were approaching the end of their careers— Norman Hunter and Terry Cooper from Leeds and Joe Royle from Manchester City. We witnessed Royle's debut for City when he scored four goals against Middlesborough. Perhaps the most memorable game came at the end of the 1977 season, the very last game. City, Coventry and Sunderland were all threatened with relegation. City were playing away at Coventry and Sunderland were playing Everton. To stay up, City needed a draw while Coventry had to win, unless Sunderland lost. As I knew Coventry well, I drove Nigel and Chris up to Highfield Road. So many City fans were travelling to the game that many could not get into the ground on time. Controversially, Coventry's managing director, the BBC pundit Jimmy Hill, requested the kick-off be delayed by 15 minutes. In a tense match, Coventry scored twice in the first half but City equalised with two goals in the second half. When news came through that Sunderland had lost 2-0, Jimmy Hill had the result announced over the tannoy. Immediately, Coventry and City stopped playing for the final 10 minutes, passing the ball backwards and forwards to each other or to their respective goalkeepers. When the full-time whistle blew both sets of fans celebrated wildly. Meanwhile, relegated Sunderland were rightly outraged by these events. After the game we went for a drink in my old local around the corner from the stadium. Under normal circumstances during the 1970s, if both sets of fans found themselves in the same pub, then a mass punch-up would inevitably ensue. But not on this night. City and Coventry fans were hugging each other, exchanging scarves and having a whale of a time.

Back at the Filton plant, I came to realise during this period that political lobbying of governments by trade unions was a distinctive feature of rank-and-file activity in the aerospace industry, something which increased greatly during the next decade. In April 1977, BAC, the Hawker Siddeley Group and Scottish Aviation were nationalised and merged by the Labour Government. The new company was renamed British Aerospace (BAe). Apart from one or two self-styled 'company men' and 'Colonel Blimps', I and many colleagues were quietly satisfied with this and viewed it as a positive consequence of electing social democratic governments which, with the exception of the 1970-74 Conservative government, much of the shop floor had experienced since 1964. Moreover, as a company that relied mostly on contracts from the British government, we supported union campaigns that put pressure on politicians to support British suppliers. During the 1980s I became actively involved in these campaigns but I had an early experience of it in 1977 and it involved classic rank-and-file militancy.

At the time, Jim Callaghan's Labour government was considering different options for the purchase of anti-tank wire-guided missile systems. One was Swingfire, designed and manufactured at BAe's Filton and Stevenage sites and the other was Milan a product of a Franco-German project named Euromissile. Expert opinion was that Milan was a superior portable system and the UK government favoured it.

The BAe unions argued that it was not just about missile systems but more importantly defending our livelihoods and supporting British manufacturing industry. The manual and non-manual unions at the Filton and Stevenage sites began plans to block major roads that passed by the plants, the A38 and A1 respectively. As was their wont, the Stevenage unions changed their minds over this at the last minute but the Filton unions (AUEW, EETPU, TGWU, AUEW-TASS and APEX) all went ahead. The action began with union members marching around the site carrying a model coffin that symbolised the threat to our factory. The blockade itself was extremely effective. Many of us took part and it resembled a large mass meeting on a main road, causing major traffic jams. Police cars were everywhere. I didn't see the particular incident but, unfortunately, it turned nasty when a car driver hit a woman called Annie MacDonald and this made the evening news. She was taken to hospital but luckily was not seriously injured. In the event, after intense lobbying, both systems were adopted.

1977-78: BICC, a two-year interlude

A month later I left BAe to start a job at BICC, the cable company. I had started to become bored with the inspection work. By that point I was still inspecting the same electronic assemblies that I had when I first moved to PSG in 1975 and I wanted something different. I applied for a job advertised at BICC's Avonmouth sales office where I was taken on as a technical sales specialist in the mineral insulated cable division, then known as BICC-Pyrotenax. Mineral insulated cable is a specialist heavy duty cable used where fire-proof wiring is required, such as in hospitals and hotels, and for underground heating and thermocouples. My role was in sales support visiting major electrical wholesalers and electrical contractors in the Wiltshire and Gloucestershire area. I was given a company car and spent my time travelling from customer to customer, promoting the products and carrying out occasional demonstrations of how to use them. I was given on-the-job training, shadowing another sales specialist, and spent two weeks at the company's Prescot factory near Liverpool, watching how the cable was made and visiting different departments. I only lasted 18 months. The problem with the job was that Wiltshire and Gloucestershire are essentially rural counties with a small number of towns such as Cheltenham and Swindon. As a result, there was never a large demand for my services and I spent a good fifty per cent of my time twiddling my thumbs or driving to destinations where not much work was required when I arrived.

The BICC office was not unionised but this time I did retain my individual membership of the EETPU. There was very little discussion of trade unionism with my colleagues, none of whom were members. During my short time there, the only contact I had with union activity was during the 1977 firefighters' strike, a nine-week dispute that was a precursor to the 1978 Winter of Discontent. James Callaghan's Labour Government had imposed a national 10% pay rise limit at a time when inflation had stood at 16%. The firefighters struck for a 30% rise. They eventually lost, though the government did concede a pay formula that brought parity with higher paid manual workers. The Avonmouth fire station was located just down the road from the BICC office and a well-supported picket line was mounted from the start of the dispute. I regularly walked down to see the pickets and to offer verbal support, contributions to the strike fund plus a bottle of whiskey on one occasion. Dressed in a suit and tie, I did not resemble a conventional union supporter and I was told that one or two of the pickets suspected I was a management spy.

The higher salary I was paid alongside Eileen's nursing shift pay, involving alternating days and nights, was useful in enabling us to put down a deposit on a three-bed terraced house in Halsbury Road, Westbury Park in 1978. We moved in during August of that year with just an old double bed, a couple of ex-RAF officer mess lounge chairs and an ancient gas stove that we purchased for £10 from a junk shop on Gloucester Road. We had plans to start a family in the near future and so I decided to return to BAe since employment there offered greater long term job security and, I hoped, more interesting work.

1979-1987: British Aerospace, before the job losses

1979-1982: Tentative activism

In December 1978 I applied for a job as a standards engineer at Filton's renamed BAe Dynamics Naval Weapons Division, which was now responsible for naval guided weapons systems along with military and civil spacecraft work, the latter forming its own division at a later stage. I was accepted and started in January. The Standards Department was housed in a very large building, known as the No1 Drawing Office, containing hundreds of draughtsmen, designers and various technical support workers. The standards engineer was responsible for drafting new, specialist engineering standards on subjects that were covered neither by the national British Standards Institution (BSI) nor the International Organisation for Standardisation (ISO). These were then referenced on engineering drawings by designers and draughtsmen.

Frequently requests would come in from the Drawing Office or a design department for a new standard to cover a particular engineering process. These could range from the rudimentary, such as deburring a metal component, to the more advanced, for example the process for utilising a particular mix of chemicals in a specialist printed circuit board manufacturing process. In cases where I did not have the knowledge nor expertise to write a detailed standard, an engineering specialist would write it for me and I would administer its approval. In other cases, where I did have such capability, I would draft the new standard and secure its approval from a range of departmental specialists across the site. Since leaving school exactly a decade earlier this was the first job I had taken on which required a clear and concise writing ability. My skill development in this respect was to prove useful in later years.

The Standards Department was comprised of a small open-plan office housing a head of department, Tony Hopton, and three standards engineers: Bob Pain, a draughtsman; Basil Simpson, a chain-smoking Irishman; and me. A couple of years later, as the department expanded, we would take on a young trainee, Robert Bone and three more standards engineers: Graham Hunter; Bob Bater, an Ecology Party (now Green Party) member and CND activist; and David McCarthy, formerly a technical college lecturer. There were also two librarians who maintained the department's large collection of national and international standards, Stan Jennings and John Vanston-Rumney,

The Standards Department, 1983. Tony Hopton presenting a gift to Stan Jennings on his retirement. I'm behind Stan on the second row.

an Irish protestant known throughout the office block affectionately as 'Paddy'. Stan and Paddy were the more interesting characters in the office. Stan was a staunch Labour Party supporter who displayed a visceral hatred of Tories and he would vent his anger on anyone who came into the office who suggested Tory leanings. During the war he was an RAF mechanic but seconded as a jeep driver to the US army in 1944. He was at the head of a column that liberated one of the Nazi death camps, an experience that on occasion he reflected on quietly. He had previously been a heavy smoker and sadly he died of lung disease not long after he retired in the mid-1980s. Paddy led a colourful life away from work. Aged in his late 50s he was a regular user of marijuana and other substances and host to all kinds of goings on in his high-rise flat in Redfield, Bristol, that are best left unreported.

The No1 Drawing Office was unionised, not 100% but to a healthily large density. Most technical staff were members of the AUEW-TASS, while clerical workers were covered by APEX, a white-collar section of the GMB. I became an AUEW-TASS member just days after joining the department. Almost immediately my union entered into a pay dispute with management. We were now at the tail end of the so-called Winter of Discontent. In the private sector many unionised firms had breached the Labour government's 5% pay limit, imposed under phase three of its Social Contract. For example, the unions at Ford had reached a 17% settlement early on. In January 1979, TGWU lorry drivers in parts of the country, including the South West, won increases of 20%. In the same month my union rejected an offer of 14% and after a mass meeting in the canteen in February, attended by over 800 members, we voted for a general overtime ban supplemented by some limited departmental strike activity. After two months of stalemate the management caved in and we accepted a 21% pay rise.

And that was not the end of it. For the first time in my life I came to learn how pay could take on a secretive, individualised property. I am referring to the system called merit pay. Each year, after the dust had settled following a pay agreement, heads of department would allocate an additional increase to those staff who, in their eyes, had performed well over the year. Most years between half to three quarters of staff might receive a rise, typically of between one to three per cent, depending on management's private assessment of performance. This system operated for technical staff at all BAe sites and many others in the industry too, such as at Rolls Royce. Its efficacy depended on individual workers keeping quiet about the outcome of the review. Some did, some didn't. Managers would discreetly hand an envelope containing details of the rise to each recipient at an opportune moment. It was of course a blue-eyed boy system, plagued by favouritism, injustice and discrimination. The site trade unions hated it because the merit pay totals ate into the overall annual budget for pay increases. Having just joined the department I received nothing, though I was handed the envelope in 1981 and '82. I shall return to the merit pay problem much later.

A general election in May 1979 resulted in the election of a Conservative Government led by Margaret Thatcher. In the aftermath of the Winter of Discontent and our experience of a Labour Government, led by a Tory-lite James Callaghan, that drifted steadily to the right during the late 1970s, this did not come as a surprise. Nevertheless, Eileen and I, our friends on the shop floor and some in my office awaited political developments with some trepidation. My mum and dad rang regularly to express their disgust. It was from this point onwards in my life that I started to become more deeply politicised, as did Eileen. We were always pretty cynical about politicians of all persuasions and, as suggested earlier, I had a problem with people in authority, as I did with the teachers in my school days. Nevertheless, I moved from a lazy assumption that social democratic government had become the norm and that a belief in the need for greater equality was growing in contemporary society—however mistaken my expectations might have been—to an understanding that people like us and the values we cherished were about to come under attack. As the Thatcher years commenced, I moved steadily towards the politics of socialism.

Later in 1979 our shop-floor unions were involved in a national dispute. These were a rarity, since plant level bargaining had long been the norm in much of the UK's engineering industry. The one exception was the regulation of the working week which at the time was the prerogative of the industry's central employer organisation, the Engineering Employers' Federation (EEF). Most manual workers in the industry worked a 40-hour week; the non-manuals worked 37 hours. The body that coordinated the engineering unions, both manual and non-manual, was the Confederation of Shipbuilding and Engineering Unions (CSEU) known colloquially as the 'Confed'. In June 1979 negotiations broke down between the CSEU and the EEF for a cut of an hour. In September, the unions launched a programme of weekly one day strikes in support of a reduction of the working week from 40 to 35 hours. At the beginning of this dispute all unions were involved, manual and non-manual. However, the timidity of the right wing CSEU leadership, dominated by the AUEW and EETPU, meant that the objectives were soon reduced in all but name to a claim for a 39-hour week. This effectively knocked out the non-manual unions. The main gates at the Filton plant were heavily picketed during these strikes and most lorry drivers were turned away. I regularly visited the pickets to talk to some of my friends, Frank Tamlyn, Chris Isaacs and Nigel Redman in particular. At its height the dispute involved 1.5 million workers and some 16 million lost working days. It was settled in October when the EEF conceded a 39-hour week, though for most workers this typically involved marginal adjustments to finishing times rather than a complete one-hour bloc. There was some talk among the non-manual unions of campaigning for an hour's cut to maintain differentials but this was not supported by the rank and file who came to accept the moral case for parity. My local AUEW-TASS union did, however, begin a discussion about the prospects for flexitime—a system that allows workers to choose when to start and end their workday within limits agreed with management—but this did not get off the ground. I mention it here because the idea was popular with members and it re-emerged in the following decade as an instrument for solving a protracted site dispute.

Another important event took place at this time. Our first daughter, Jessica, was born on November 26th. I was present at the birth, a truly emotional experience and a personal challenge since I've never liked the sight of blood and always felt uncomfortable in hospitals. Embarrassing as this is, I have to admit that as a boy I once passed out during a TV episode of Dr Kildare. Eileen, however, was made of stronger stuff and although she was in labour for quite some time, the birth was straightforward. Clearly parenting was now our main priority in life. Eileen took maternity leave for the first eleven weeks and then decided to resign from her work. I was granted a week's discretionary leave. On my return, rather than plan a shift in my work-life balance, I found that I had to put in extra overtime hours in the office. This was a direct result of the economic policies of the new government. Greatly influenced by the work of Friedrich Hayek and Milton Friedman, Thatcher and her chancellor Geoffrey Howe began a policy of spending cuts and money supply reduction to control inflation. One of the prime levers for the latter was interest rates. In the same month as Jessica was born, Bank of England interest rates were increased to 17%, compared to 11% earlier in the year. This was pretty catastrophic for young homeowners with large mortgages. At certain points I wondered whether we would have to sell up. My only option was to work as much overtime as I could get, meaning most evenings and Saturday mornings. This did help financially but of course it meant excessive housework for Eileen. The situation did not change until a year later when our second daughter arrived. Not long after this Eileen returned to nursing, working part-time weekend shifts, and, whilst she was working, I took over childcare duties.

Thus, through 1980, the pattern in our lives, as with most young parents, was the pleasure—and toil—of childcare mixed with lengthy paid working hours. This intensified at the end of November 1980 when Detta was born. Some quizzed us, and still do, about our choice of name. It can be a shortened version of Odette, Claudette, and most commonly Bernadette which is her name. The name has French and German origins and means as strong as a bear. Despite its association with miracle working Catholic saints, it was always one of my favourite girls' names. The first vinyl single I bought was Bernadette by the Four Tops and that always stuck with me; and one of the politicians I most admired at that time in the context of the Troubles was Bernadette

Devlin. We both saw nothing wrong with the name and I maintain to this day that such an elegant name should be re-appropriated from its religious associations. But we knew that when she went to school her friends were bound to call her Bernie which we did not like, so we called her Detta from the beginning.

Worries about the type of future our two daughters would grow up in, indeed whether they would have a future at all, were the catalyst for our decision to join CND in 1981. This was the period when the Cold War between NATO countries and the Soviet Union was intensifying. The Conservative government was planning to replace the Polaris submarine fleet with Trident missiles—a clear escalation of the arms race—and women began blockading the RAF Greenham Common base in protest at the government's decision to allow the USA to station Cruise missiles at the site. On 24th October 1981 we travelled to London to join 250,000 protestors marching for unilateral nuclear disarmament. Both the Labour leader Michael Foot and Tony Benn spoke at the rally. It was the first time I had witnessed a Benn speech. Little did I know that it would be the first of many over the coming years. Two years later, on 22nd October 1983, we both took part in another huge CND march in London of over one million people. This time the new Labour leader Neil Kinnock spoke passionately for unilateral nuclear disarmament. It would only be another four years before he dropped the policy.

The early 1980s were the period of Tory privatisations, notably of companies such as Cable and Wireless, Jaguar, British Telecom, Britoil, British Gas and later British Steel, British Petroleum, Rolls Royce, British Airways and the water and electricity utilities. Politicians such as Thatcher, Geoffrey Howe and Keith Joseph prepared the electorate for this, arguing that the discipline of the market would make the firms more productive. The Labour Party and trade union movement opposed the policy but in the absence of specific militant action the opposition was ineffective. The first company to be privatised, in February 1981, was my own employer British Aerospace, when nearly 52% of shares were sold, with the remainder in 1985. The accompanying Tory propaganda put great stress on the creation of a shareholding democracy and for this privatisation each employee was given £50 worth of shares. Most union members sold them immediately, as did I. The BAe CSEU unions organised a national march of opposition in London, which I took part in, but there were no further actions.

CSEU march against BAe privatisation, Hyde Park, 1981.

1982 was the year in which I took the first step in becoming more active in my union. Initially, I was not particularly interested in AUEW-TASS. Coming from a shop-floor union, I felt that non-manual union membership did not offer the strength and solidarity seen on the shop floor. The non-manuals were perceived as less militant and prone to watching the negotiations and industrial actions of their manual counterparts, then demanding the same settlement once the manuals had done all the hard work. Frank Tamlyn told me later that on more than one occasion he had referred to the non-manual unions at mass meetings as "the pimps and parasites, they haven't gone in yet but they will do!" Despite this, my growing political awareness, exemplified by the decision to join CND and a growing abhorrence of the new Tory government, was catalysing a feeling that I should get up off my feet and participate in whatever way I could in the growing opposition to the Tories and their supporters, known then as the New Right.

I began making enquiries about the union with reps in the Drawing Office. I was already aware that Ken Gill, the General Secretary of AUEW-TASS, was a leading member of the British Communist Party and I did wonder at the time about the contradiction between this and the perception of his members as being typically non-militant and certainly not left wing in outlook. The union had its origins in the Association of Engineering and Shipbuilding Draughtsmen (AESD) which was founded just before the outbreak of World War One. This was a small, exclusive craft union comprising mostly draughtsmen and led in the main by an unaccountable right-wing leadership. For most of its history it was not a militant union though, during the 1950s, as the economy expanded, shop-floor worker militancy generated significant wage increases. Fearing a loss of wage differentials, AESD increasingly fought annual wage claims with industrial action and as a result its membership grew substantially, incorporating a growing number of technician occupations outside of the Drawing Office. As a result, the union changed its name to the Draughtsmen's and Allied Technicians' Association (DATA). In 1970, DATA formed a section within the new Amalgamated Union of Engineering Workers and was called AUEW-TASS (Technical and Supervisory Section). In 1974, Ken Gill, who had previously been an AESD divisional organiser in Liverpool and subsequently a Deputy General Secretary, was appointed General Secretary. This reflected the growing influence of the Broad Left—which I shall come to shortly—as the complexion of the union leadership and bureaucracy shifted markedly to the left.[4]

In March 1982, a month before the outbreak of the Falklands War, I became an AUEW-TASS Corresponding Member for my Standards Department and the adjoining Configuration Department which contained around fifty white collar workers checking project drawing configuration, correct versions, amendments and so on. The Corresponding Member was a relatively minor role, supporting the local union representative in circulating union information and clarifying news on union negotiations where necessary. It was essentially a first step to becoming a full representative.

The period of the Falklands War was difficult for anyone working in an arms factory who opposed it. I and some of my colleagues were shocked by the sinking of the Belgrano. The sombre mood in the offices worsened when HMS Sheffield was subsequently sunk and the lugubrious Ministry of Defence spokesperson, Ian McDonald, announced daily casualties on the TV news. The atmosphere became at times oppressive and the critical discussions I took part in were marked by secretive whispering in corners of the office much of the time. The Labour Party leadership supported the conflict and most trade unions acquiesced through silence, as did my union. When unlimited overtime was offered to hundreds of shop floor workers and design engineers working on Sea

4 B. Parkin, The Broad Left in TASS, International Socialism, No.74, January 1975, pp.16-19.

Dart, Sea Wolf and Rapier missile systems, union concerns were raised that they were working themselves out of jobs. But such opposition was muted. Back at home, Eileen was also firmly against the war and at the same time worried about her brother Derek who was a sailor on the Ark Royal.

In the Spring I started to attend my union branch meetings, AUEW-TASS Bristol No 4 Branch. These were held monthly at 5.30pm in the Horseshoe Inn just around the corner from one of the factory's main gates on the A38. Typical agendas comprised motions submitted by members, most often activists, reports of plant negotiations, activity of the national union, reports from local Labour Party and Trades Council delegates and correspondence, which itself opened up discussions on appeals from other trade union campaigns, political organisations, and so on. The meetings were not attended by many rank-and-file union members; most were office representatives or those holding a branch position. Numbers were small, the most I ever saw there being little more than twenty out of a membership at that time of nearly 1,000. However, this did make for greater intimacy and I got to know the leading branch officials fairly quickly. I gradually came to realise that the act of participating in union affairs was not just a process of rank-and-file democracy but equally one of learning the skills of speaking in public and thinking about political issues through discursive reasoning. I did not find this easy at first. With friends and colleagues I could be as outspoken as anyone but faced with strangers I tended to clam up. The first time I stood up to make a point at a branch meeting I was nervous and no doubt a bit incoherent. But I gradually got used to it and by the time, in later years, I had to address mass meetings, conferences or speak to the media, I became far more confident. I have always thought that, apart from everything else, trade union activism provides working-class people a wonderful education in the art of speaking in public with confidence.

The early 1980s saw significant advances in the development of computer technologies and particularly their application to manufacturing industry. One of the more prominent innovations in engineering was the design of software for computer-aided design and computer-aided manufacturing (CAD-CAM, later known as CADAM). A common problem was that engineers rarely paid sufficient attention to the practical difficulties of manufacturing their designs on the shop floor. CAD-CAM offered the prospect of better integration between design and production. Fully integrated CADAM came later but in the early period, drawing office managers throughout much of the sector sought to introduce CAD hardware. The reaction of many draughtsmen was one of alarm and opposition. The fear was that CAD, by simplifying, standardising and speeding up the design process, would yield greater control to management and cause eventual job losses. Equally, the craft and skill that goes into producing a drawing by hand, the more complex of which required a good deal of technical artistry, would be replaced by the software's armoury of standard calculations and draughting routines. In other words, notwithstanding the new computer skills required to work with CAD, the overall effect would be a degradation of skills.

These were the concerns of many draughtsmen in the No1 Drawing Office. When management attempted to introduce the technology along with staff training programmes in 1982, the office's AUEW-TASS section voted to oppose it and to impose an overtime ban if the company persevered. Management then suspended its plans but examples of the hardware and software were left in place to allow the draughtsmen to 'play' with the equipment if they so wished. This was seen as a ploy to gradually weaken the opposition and very few did so. However, eventually the departmental union reps did agree to enter into negotiations and after many months an agreement was reached late in 1982. One of the national union recommendations on this issue was that negotiators should seek a reduction in working hours to guard against potential job losses. The Bristol management and their counterparts in the many other BAe plants across the country refused to concede this, on the grounds that changes to the working week were the sole prerogative of the EEF, which regulated hours across the whole industry. Individual companies could not opt out of this control. Thus, disappointingly, the final agreement did not incorporate reductions in hours, but instead granted a pay increase of 6% to all re-trained draughtsmen along with guarantees that no job losses would result from the use of the equipment. Ironically, two years later, AUEW-TASS members at Westland Helicopter plants in Weston-super-Mare and Yeovil went on strike to oppose the imposition of shift working with the use of CAD technology. Although an eventual settlement included double day shift work, they succeeded in securing a 32½ hour working week for affected workers. The EEF conceded this because contractual hours normally changed to fit shift work patterns. The convenor, Jim Black, who I came to know well, was, nevertheless, rightly proud of a significant achievement. Eight years later, the plant was closed. Jim retrained as a maths teacher and got a job at a local secondary school.

Later in the year, on 22nd September 1982, the TUC called a day of action in support of NHS workers who had been in dispute with the government over pay since May. The NHS unions demanded a 12% pay rise against the government's offer of 6% and embarked upon a programme of one-day strikes and actions short of a strike during the summer months. They were supported by sporadic sympathy strikes by miners, shipbuilders, printers and workers from local government, amongst others. These were the days when trade unions were quite prepared to break the government's anti-trade union laws—sympathy strikes having been greatly restricted by the 1980 Employment Act. The TUC's National Day of Action aimed to place further pressure on the government. The manual and non-manual unions from both BAe Filton plants—Commercial Aircraft and Naval Weapons—organised a mass meeting in the morning, followed by a TUC union march in Bristol and a strike for the remainder of the day. I attended the mass meeting and was pleased to see Tony Benn on the platform, who predictably gave a stirring speech in solidarity with low-paid NHS workers. The mass meeting and Bristol rally were well supported but the BAe Naval Weapons contingent was dominated by manual workers, probably three quarters of the total present. This was to give me a flavour of the challenges to come for organising different groups of white-collar workers.

1983: In at the deep end

Two developments of note occurred in 1983. First, Eileen and I both joined the Labour Party and I soon became a party activist. Second, I became greatly involved in union activity. We joined the Labour Party for emotional reasons as much as anything. It was at the time of the 1983 general election and political opinion, backed up by the polls, was that the Party was heading for a heavy defeat. A major contributory factor was the defection in 1981 of some leading right-wing Labour politicians such as David Owen, Roy Jenkins and Shirley Williams to the newly formed Social Democratic Party (SDP), thus splitting the opposition to the Conservatives. Another was mainstream media representations of a deep divide in the Labour Party with the Bennite left pitched against the Denis Healy-led right, with Michael Foot, the leader, attempting to survive in the middle. But for us, the main reason was that Margaret Thatcher, by now the subject of our visceral hatred, was winning popular support across the country for reasons not solely connected to the Falklands War. So with a growing sense of despair, we joined in the hope that we could contribute practical support to Party activity in our area. By this time, I had become a strong supporter of the policies of Tony Benn, one of our Bristol MPs. I went to his election meetings in the city. I devoured his books, Arguments for Socialism and Arguments for Democracy, and came to believe that there is a route to socialism that does not necessarily entail violent revolution. In later years I would be exposed to arguments from fellow union activists, members of the Socialist Workers Party, Militant Tendency and various small communist parties, that capitalism cannot be fundamentally changed or defeated by social democratic parties no matter how radical their policies. But I was pessimistic about politics then (and still am) and could not envisage the emergence of conditions in the UK, in many respects a deeply conservative country, that might give rise to widespread support for revolutionary politics. Indeed, I always felt that if there were to be a revolution it was more likely to come from the right than the left.

So we joined the Labour Party. We were given membership cards (I still have mine) on which were printed the Constitution of The Labour Party Clause IV (4):

> To secure for the workers by hand or by brain the full fruits of their industry and the most equal distribution thereof that may be possible upon the basis of the common ownership of the means of production, distribution and exchange, and the best obtainable system of popular administration and control of each industry or service.

These were sacred words for many Party members, they were for me. It wasn't until much later when Tony Blair ditched Clause IV that I resigned.[5]

I did some canvassing for Pam Tatlow, our Bristol West candidate, during the election, an activity I enjoyed and have done many times since. I found it uplifting to meet people of like minds on the doorstep, who often gave me a very warm welcome. They reminded you that you were not alone. Others of course were Tories and occasionally there

---

5 I rejoined in 2015 when Jeremy Corbyn was elected leader.

would be heated arguments. Then there were the difficult ones like the lifelong Labour supporters who demanded that we bring back hanging. The constituency was won by the Tory, William Waldegrave, the 12th Earl of Waldegrave and, of course, Eton educated. He beat into second place the Liberal candidate, George Ferguson (who much later became an elected Bristol mayor and, in my opinion, made a hash of it). Pam Tatlow came third. In the country, Margaret Thatcher won a landslide majority of 144.

Later in the year I was persuaded to become Chair of my local Henleaze Labour Party and was duly elected at the AGM. I had been a member for little more than six months! I suppose it is not unusual for fresh faces to be elected to such positions when the old guard become tired of doing the work and are keen to give way.

The second round of developments were more significant for their impact upon my working life and indeed, life at home. Early in 1983, the union rep for my area (comprising around 70 members) decided to stand down and asked me to take his place. I needed little persuasion to accept. A request for nominations was sent to all members and my name was the only one put forward. I was elected unopposed. Little more than a month later my union branch secretary, a production planner named Paul Skinner, decided to stand down and asked me to consider standing for the position. I agreed and again was elected unopposed.

Perhaps at this point I should explain the structure and mechanics of my union's method of representation. Collective bargaining in most companies in the UK's engineering sector was carried out at the plant level. That is, national level negotiations of the form that are more common in the public sector were a rarity and restricted solely to changes in working hours. Thus, at BAe, most negotiations were the prime responsibility of rank-and-file union activists. When I myself became involved in negotiations I soon discovered that as far as the employer was concerned such plant autonomy was a mirage.

The core unit of rank-and-file representation was either a discrete department or a group of workers with the same occupation but spread over a number of offices. At our plant, just under 1,000 members were spread across 21 such units, defined and agreed with our industrial relations management. Members in each unit or office elected a union rep to sit on the Joint Office Committee (JOC). The 21 JOC reps met monthly and discussed all industrial relations matters appertaining to any specific office or across the whole site. It had the prime responsibility of approving pay claims and other initiatives, voting on recommendations to enter into disputes with management, sanctioning proposals for industrial action and agreeing on recommendations to end disputes. In addition, rank-and-file members elected 12 health and safety reps every year, each responsible for monitoring health and safety issues in their areas of work. The actual process of negotiation with management was the responsibility of the site Negotiating Committee. This comprised six members elected from the JOC. The Negotiating Committee met management at least monthly to discuss routine industrial relations issues and more frequently during pay talks or, later in the decade, redundancies. The Negotiating Committee reported to the JOC each month. The JOC and the Negotiating Committee each elected a chair and secretary every year. The chair and secretary of the Negotiating Committee were designated the site senior reps.

Between them, the JOC and Negotiating Committee gave regular reports of their activity to monthly branch meetings. These, along with mass meetings of the whole membership, afforded rank-and-file members the opportunity to participate in discussions and decisions on all plant industrial relations matters.

Not long after I was elected Branch Secretary, I was also elected JOC Secretary. Within 12 months of taking on the role of Corresponding Member in 1982, I had become a union activist with a growing workload. I enjoyed this work immensely. My role was to keep the rank-and-file organisation operating smoothly by writing reports, newsletters, minutes and so on and by taking a full, often leading part in union discussions. I was also required to liaise regularly with the AUEW-TASS regional officers.

There were three regional officers responsible for members in the South West, though their number would increase in coming years as the union embarked on a policy of expansion by merger. They were all based in an office in Coldharbour Road, Redland, just a five-minute walk from our house. I would get to work with them pretty closely in the coming years. Dave Yeomans, a Brummie, was a hardline communist and strong supporter of the Morning Star faction. He was responsible for union members at Rolls Royce in Bristol and other manufacturing firms in the region. Charles Lomas was a Scouser and Labour Party member with links to many MPs and party officials. A Bennite, he was also a Morning Star supporter. He covered firms in the Gloucestershire area, such as Dowty Aerospace and Smith's Industries. Derek Perkins, from the Black Country, was the official I worked most closely with. Another hardline communist, again aligned with the Morning Star faction—as were most AUEW-TASS officials by now—he was the most charismatic of the three. He was responsible for BAe and the Westland Helicopter plants in the South West, amongst others. He was a powerful speaker and often scintillating in his sardonic wit at meetings between our Negotiating Committee and the EEF on the occasions when plant negotiations had broken down. He never once tried to engineer weaker settlements behind our backs, which was a common fault of too many officials of British unions seeking a quiet life. He did not, however, suffer fools gladly and his temper was such that many on his own side were always wary of him. I got on well with him though and he appreciated the work we were doing at the plant. The only time he lost his temper with me was during the Westland affair in 1985-86 when the Tory cabinet was split over whether to sanction a rescue bid for the ailing company from the Italian firm Agusta or the American Sikorsky. The rival bids were to be put to a vote at a special shareholders' meeting. I had a letter published in the Guardian and Bristol Evening Post calling for the workers to decide the issue by ballot. The Evening Post made it their lead letter with a large headline. In this I wrote,

> But I find it very sad that throughout the current crisis nobody has seen fit to ask the workforce for its views on how the problems can be resolved—or even, dare I say it, offer them a vote. Do the views of thousands of workers who have invested years of their lives in the company count for nothing?[6]

This was not in line with Ken Gill's public statements and Derek Perkins was pretty livid.

It was Derek Perkins, who, in 1983, invited me to join the AUEW-TASS Broad Left. He said that it was formed of groups of likeminded TASS activists and officials in each region of the country who met regularly to discuss union policy and elections outside of the formal union structure. By 'likeminded' he meant individuals who supported 'progressive policies'. He used this term repeatedly. I soon came to understand that it meant adopting the Communist Party's industrial strategy without actually mentioning the name of the party, so as not to attract the attention of unsympathetic rank-and-file members. Why? Because the

---

6 *Bristol Evening Post*, 'Ask the workers about the future of Westland', 2 January 1986.

industrial strategy was to ensure that sufficient numbers of Communist Party members (along with a minority of trusted left-wing Labour Party members) were elected to key positions of influence at local and national levels. By doing so, the union was to become firmly embedded on the left of the political spectrum of the British labour movement.

The Broad Left developed in the original AESD union during the late 1950s and 1960s in the context of a union led by right-wing officials that were incapable of supporting the struggles of its members. The AESD draughtsmen were becoming increasingly militant in response to the drift in wage differentials caused by the successful wage campaigns of the engineering manual unions in this period. The nascent Broad Left, comprising a small number of officials but growing number of rank-and-file left-wing Labour members and Communist Party members, was able to mobilise opposition to the union leadership. Gradually many AESD branches and divisional councils were taken over by Broad Left members. Once in a position of strength they then concentrated on winning key elections at the annual Representative Council Conference, where crucial posts such as President and members of the Standing Orders Committee and Selection Committee for Appointment of Full Time Officials were elected. By the 1970s, the Broad Left seemed in total control of the new union, AUEW-TASS. The General Secretary, Ken Gill, was a Communist Party member as were over 60% of the union's full-time officials. The National Executive Committee and delegates to the annual conference were dominated by the Broad Left.[7]

I decided to become a regular participant. By 1983, at the time Derek Perkins asked me to join, the Broad Left had come to completely dominate the union. The culture and outlook of the organisation, what these days people refer to annoyingly in marketing-speak as 'the brand', was referred to regularly by the national press as 'TASS, the left-wing union led by the Communist Ken Gill.' Having previously been a member of the EETPU, which was referred to regularly as 'the right-wing union led by the scourge of the left Frank Chapple', I was more than comfortable with the left-wing label, indeed, proud to be an activist with such a union. It was once I had become fully acquainted with the mechanics of policy-making that I gradually became a little irritated with some of the antics of the Communist Party members.

The Bristol Broad Left meetings were held monthly at a civil service club in the Old Market area of the city and comprised typically around

---

7 B. Parkin, The Broad Left in TASS, International Socialism, No.74, January 1975, pp.16-19.

50 members. This is now a bistro bar. Critics of the Broad Left would often assume that these meetings merely rubber-stamped and put into action the commands issuing from the top of the union. This was partly true but not totally so. For sure, each meeting would hear a report and recommendations from Peter Luck, our National Executive Committee member, on behalf of the national committee of the Broad Left, itself headed in all but name by Ken Gill. Moreover, we all respected our full-time officials, Derek Perkins, Dave Yeomans and Charles Lomas, and we regularly followed their lead in articulating and supporting Broad Left positions. But there could often be heated discussions and dissent emanating, in particular from Labour Party members in the group and some communists too. Most of the Labour contingent were left-wing members like me, including at least two Militant Tendency supporters. Another, Mike Parker, a friend of mine from my plant, was a member of the Socialist Workers' Party. One example of dissent that I remember well, and I apologise here for jumping forward in time, was the Communist Party's strong support for retaining and expanding nuclear power in the UK's energy sector at a time when many left-wing Labour Party MPs and activists rejected this. We were asked to endorse the Communist Party line because of the number of union jobs concentrated in the nuclear sector. But of course, these jobs could easily be transferred to alternative modes of generating electricity. The real reason for the Communist Party's position was that nuclear power was integral to the Soviet Union's energy industry. It all came to a head during one Broad Left meeting in 1986, just months after the Chernobyl disaster. The national Broad Left instructed us to vote for an annual conference motion supporting nuclear power in the UK. Following an angry discussion led by the non-Communist Party contingent, we voted to reject the recommendation and to vote against the motion at conference.

What is certainly true of the Communist Party domination of the Broad Left is the condescension and occasional animosity directed at any Trotskyist members and other outright dissidents, both in group meetings and at the annual conference. Members of Trotskyist organisations were regarded as irritants and often marginalised. Whilst I occasionally found some appeal in their oft-stated predictions of widespread revolutionary activity among the working class that would bring an end to the capitalist order, I also knew that such ideas were hopelessly lacking in evidence of its prospects. This was no reason to ignore their contributions, however. Indeed, it has to be said that at no time can I remember our Communist Party members discussing the prospects for revolution or even the prospects for democratic socialism, or what these might look like. Many of them were great industrial organisers but they preferred to leave political discussion within the boundaries of Labour Party discourse. Their problem was that they did not like free thinkers or certainly those whose views contradicted their party policy.

1984: A full time activist, the miners' strike and a plant occupation

Returning now to industrial relations at BAe, at the end of 1983 I was voted on to the site negotiating committee and elected as secretary. Alongside the chair, Alan Stevens, I was now the site's senior AUEW-TASS representative, working more or less full time on union matters.

We had six reps on the committee. These were Richard Clatworthy and Phil 'Spider' Harrison from the Test Department, Kate Kelliher a graduate engineer and women's representative, Steve Baldock from the Drawing Office, Alan Stevens, another graduate engineer and myself. On occasion we would face the top brass, various company directors, for consultative meetings or where industrial disputes required their intervention. Our regular meetings were with the opposing team of industrial relations managers, all based in the Personnel Department, who would often be accompanied by a senior manager from one of the site office departments. Ernie Peck was the lead management negotiator, a man we argued with relentlessly and who rarely strayed from the company line. Nevertheless, of all the managers we faced he was the one we trusted most. We might incessantly disagree but, whenever he did concede anything, he kept his word. Another was Mike John, an ex-TASS rep himself. He often positioned himself as quietly sympathetic to trade unions and thus the soft cop in the management set up. We rarely took him seriously. The tough cop was a younger manager named Malcolm Fiddler. He was destined to climb the management ladder (years later he became a senior human resources manager at Airbus). I came to understand that many of our routine negotiating meetings were mere games in which one side (management) were the refuseniks (unless they wanted something) and the other side (us) were intent on getting them to lose their tempers by drilling into their weak spots. By nature I have always been quite a placid character, not easily upset, and I enjoyed watching the other side lose their tempers when their threats and caustic remarks were met with no more than smiles and laughter on our side. In one spell of anger, one manager mentioned the Economic League, the blacklisting agency, and, by implication, his support of it. I thought afterwards that if my name was on the list then at least I would have achieved something in my life.

These observations need to be understood in the context of the reality of plant-based bargaining at BAe. In theory, management at each plant had autonomy over industrial relations issues. Equally, the expectation of the unions was that when we submitted claims, we expected meaningful negotiations with those managers and little interference from corporate headquarters when agreements were reached. This was how things worked out when the issues were entirely local, such as a new grading scheme in a particular office, or a departmental union recognition claim. However, for pay and conditions—holidays, working time and so on—although plant management would not admit to it, all the strings were pulled by company directors at the various BAe headquarters. I recently listened to a Radio 4 documentary about diplomatic relations with China. One UK diplomat said that the Chinese way of negotiating never shifted. It was like negotiating with a brick wall. Whatever the proposal or issue, the negotiators would give no response until they had returned from their leaders with an answer. And so it was at BAe. Decentralised negotiations with a centralised management. Only rarely were we able to break this down, normally during a dispute involving industrial action that hurt the company.

I tried to address this problem during pay negotiations early in 1984, only months after joining the negotiating committee. A routine pay dispute had fizzled out with an unsatisfactory, albeit above inflation, pay rise following a brief work to rule. Disconcerted by our management's inability to negotiate independently, I submitted a motion to my branch that called on the national union to campaign for national negotiations at BAe. I had been appointed as the Bristol delegate to the AUEW-TASS National Aerospace Committee. It met twice yearly at the union head office in Richmond-upon-Thames and comprised delegates from over 12 BAe UK plants. The committee was led by Chris Darke, the union's national officer for the aerospace sector. A Eurocommunist, he was not completely on Ken Gill's wavelength. We all trusted him, however, since we recognised the huge amount of work he put into campaigning on behalf of workers in the industry. Chris was sympathetic to my motion but doubted it would pass. He was right. Although it did attract some support, two vociferous delegates from the large Warton and Kingston plants felt that the status quo was preferable, on the basis that if the more militant plants won larger settlements, on pay for instance, then the other plants could queue up for parity. Some good did come out of the discussion in that we agreed that each year Chris Darke and his head office researchers would produce detailed analysis of company accounts and other economic factors enabling the plants to generate similar pay claims and arguments to support them. With its distinctive blue cover, it became known as the Blue Book.

I cannot remember a major claim at my plant that did not result in a breakdown in plant negotiations after all internal stages in our disputes procedure had been exhausted. In such situations we would register a 'failure to agree'. This triggered what was called a Works Conference, where the two opposing teams of negotiators would be joined by their respective external full-time officials. The conference was sometimes held at the Filton site or occasionally at the Engineering Employers Federation (EEF) Bristol headquarters at Engineers House along the Promenade in Clifton. This was a Grade II listed mansion built by Charles Pinney who was mayor of Bristol during the Bristol Riots of 1831. When we arrived, we would sometimes enjoy upsetting the secretaries by announcing loudly that "when the revolution comes all this will be ours" as we were led through the building. On the management side there was an individual representing the EEF and on our side our own full time official, Derek Perkins. We used to enjoy watching Derek, with his acerbic Black Country wit, destroy the arguments of the public-school voices coming from the other side. Of course, once again it was only theatre since at its conclusion the conference would never end with a settlement. It was merely a final stage that allowed management to see if we were prepared to take industrial action or not.

Whether we were prepared to take action depended on a number of factors. First, unlike our manual workers, and with the exception of the CAD new technology dispute, the non-manual workforce was rarely confronted with management attempts to exert more control over patterns of work. In that respect, as long as we completed our various tasks in acceptable time (in those days in the aerospace industry time was pretty elastic), we were left alone by our supervisers. Moreover, none of us had experienced any form of mass redundancy for decades.

And so the remaining issue that did regularly generate conflict was the annual pay award. The UK's aerospace sector was well known for its pay disputes where both sides fought hard to retain the upper hand.[8] Our Filton site had its fair share of these, especially in the late 1970s and the 1980s, when management felt emboldened by the political environment to tighten their control of labour costs.

Second, again unlike the manual workforce, we were well aware that taking all-out strike action rarely had any immediate negative effect on our employer compared to the costs incurred by our members. When the manual unions went on strike, production halted and products ceased going out from the factory gates. When our union went on strike, it was certainly a problem for management but the cessation of producing designs, drawings and associated design support work could only have a longer-term effect. Our strategy, and it was replicated at many other BAe sites, was to box clever wherever we could. If we went into dispute, we would often impose a work to rule, a go-slow and an overtime ban. The buoyant nature of work in the aerospace and defence sectors during this period meant that these actions, when taken together, and if maintained for long enough, could be a cost-effective way of hurting management sufficiently to secure a new offer. Many of our members took the working to rule seriously. They might temporarily lose drawings and paperwork, work at a more leisurely pace, or go for walks around the plant. Considering the size of the plant, with an airfield large enough to cater for Concorde and the monster Brabazon aircraft, this meant that the keenest walkers could be gone for hours.

Nevertheless, if we needed to attempt to bring matters to a head, we would strike. In 1987 we organised a series of strikes, which I detail further below. However, a more common method was the use of sectional strikes. By this I mean taking out some key departments where the stoppage of work might be more keenly felt by management, rather than an all-out strike, which of course lowers pay costs in the short term. Departments selected might include: a particularly busy project group in the Drawing Office; the Estimating Department where projects were costed, the stopping of which immediately affected the customer; the Mainframe Computer Department; or the test engineers whose absence would indeed cause a halt to the flow of production. Support for such action would be taken by a show of hands in each department and then a levy would be imposed on the remaining membership to compensate

---

8 B. Wooton, Incomes Policy, London: Davis-Poynter, 1974.

the strikers. This strategy was used successfully in our 1980 pay dispute, the year we won a 21% rise. It was used again in 1985 during a short dispute, less wholeheartedly supported, when we accepted a rise well short of our objectives, and again in 1987.

The third factor which we had to take into account was again specific to the non-manual unions. If the manual unions embarked upon some form of industrial action, they were bound to have a handful of members who disagreed with it but due to the closed shop agreement on the shop floor, none could resign. In the non-manual areas we had no such agreement. In our disputes we often had a small but significant minority of members who disagreed with the proposed action, some of whom would resign from the union. As the branch secretary for much of the 1980s, I was the one who received these resignations and, if I received too many, in excess of ten, I would start to lose sleep at night because I knew Derek Perkins would be after me. On the other hand, we would normally recruit some new members during our disputes, those who were becoming disaffected with management and supported the TASS position, and if these were sufficient to nullify the effect of the resignations, I would be happy.

So, with careful consideration of these issues, each year the TASS Joint Office Committee of union reps would discuss the merits of a sizeable pay claim, and, in our sure knowledge that management would throw it out, whether or not there was sufficient support and determination to win a dispute without too much damage in terms of membership loss on our side.

Almost immediately after our 1984 pay claim was settled, developments in the UK's coal mining industry were to have a significant impact on my union and Labour Party work. On 6th March, Ian MacGregor, a Scottish-American industrialist appointed by Thatcher to head the National Coal Board, announced that twenty collieries would close, involving the loss of some 20,000 jobs out of a total of a little over 170,000. The miners' leader, Arthur Scargill, predicted at the time that the government really wanted to close 70 pits. The government denied this, though in the end Scargill's prediction was an underestimate. There followed the national miners' strike which lasted precisely twelve months.

For the first couple of months of the strike, my support activity was restricted to participation in debates at various levels of the local Labour Party and at my local TASS Bristol No 4 Branch. Support for the strike was solid in both, but excessive time was taken up with the angst articulated by the more lukewarm supporters who felt that the NUM should have held a national ballot. I was quite animated by this. As far as I was concerned, this was an irritating distraction from the key issue of how capitalism creates industrial communities dependent on single employers, exploits them, and once they've served their purpose abandons them to a future of life on the dole. In any case, it was the prerogative of the elected leadership of the NUM to assess their members' support for the strike and how it should be prosecuted. As there was widespread opposition to the government's anti-union legislation in the labour movement, I joined the many comrades who argued that it was hypocritical for other union members or Labour Party members to effectively endorse the Tory government's condemnation of the lack of a national ballot. The government had already announced legislation making strike ballots compulsory that year. Many of us rejected this. My view was that to vote for a strike by a show of hands at a mass meeting was an act of true collectivism, of visible solidarity. To do so in the privacy of the home was an act of individualised choice, a process that would inevitably weaken a union's attempt to mobilise its members.

The argument never died down entirely but by the early summer of 1984 it became clear that our hopes for an early miners' victory were unfounded. Thatcher's strategy, of stockpiling coal in advance of the strike, of arranging cheap coal imports and of imposing an effective police state to render miners' flying pickets ineffective, meant that this was bound to be a long, difficult dispute. And so, just as in many other parts of the country, the labour movement in Bristol set into motion a network of miners' support groups. These were coordinated by the Bristol Miners' Support Campaign Group which was led by a young Labour Councillor called Dawn Primarolo (the chair) and Ron Thomas, the left-wing Labour MP who lost his Bristol North West seat in the 1979 general election (the treasurer). Ron seemed to me to be the guy doing most of the work behind the scenes.

I did attend one or two meetings of the campaign group, but to be honest I devoted most of my time to coordinating support activity in the strongly Tory area of Henleaze, Bristol. I was already chair of Henleaze Labour Party and I duly volunteered to take the role of miners' support coordinator. Our main effort was to set up a regular collection of food and money outside the decidedly middle-class Waitrose supermarket on Henleaze Road. Every Saturday, and on some evenings of the week, we arranged for volunteers to stand outside the main entrance of the shop. Normally there would be around six of us, about the size of a modern-day union picket! We stood outside in rain or sunshine, armed with posters and leaflets and with boxes to collect food donations. We also collected money. Jack Evans, an old communist, and father of one of our local Labour councillors, Judy Patterson, always brought along a bucket adorned with the Morning Star logo. He was a colourful character and successful in getting a fair few doubtful shoppers, as well as the sympathetic ones, to donate to the cause.

I would estimate that something like one in five of the shoppers donated small amounts of food or money at each collection. Not bad considering the political hue of the area: a lot of blue and quite a lot of yellow too. We did encounter some moments of tension, however. When the Ethiopian famine was brought to national attention by the BBC reporter Michael Buerk in October 1984, we had a period when angry individuals would come up to us and scream that we were collecting for undeserving union militants rather than the starving millions. And we endured the same treatment when, in November 1984, the Welsh taxi driver David Wilkie, carrying a working miner, was killed when two striking miners dropped a concrete block from a footbridge on the M4. The most bizarre incident occurred in the summer when a small group of young local Tories, led by a blonde woman dressed up in Nazi regalia, proceeded to goose-step in front of us. Our takings increased that day.

At home, I still have copies of all receipts of monies collected that I paid to the Bristol Miners' Support Campaign Group, along with the City Council's permit for street collection and Ron Thomas's letter confirming that I was an official collector. Why do I still have them? I suppose it's because I have hidden them away since October 1984, when I received a phone call from Ron, advising that the courts had authorised the sequestration of NUM funds following the union's refusal to pay a £200,000 fine for non-compliance with a balloting ruling. He asked me to hide all records of the money collected. He also warned that it was likely that my home phone would be tapped. You can call it paranoia but for a period following this our home phone did indeed start to make clear clicking noises each time I answered the phone or made a call. This happened again a few years later when I was involved in two major union disputes at Filton.

For the record, the total monies collected by my Henleaze support group between 15th June 1984 and 28th February 1985 amounted to

South Wales NUM poster on sequestration, one of
many displayed in our Filton union office.

£3,481.99 (around £11,270 in today's money). This included £336.87 collected during the 1984 Christmas week. During the same period, we also collected large quantities of food, the value of which was not calculated. The food collections came under the remit of Bristol West Constituency Labour Party, which was twinned with a pit village, Penrhiwceiber, in the Cynon Valley, an area renowned for the militancy of the pits. Regularly Bristol West volunteers drove to the village at weekends to deliver the donations to miners and their wives at the union lodge hall.

I managed to go on a couple of these visits, but by now much of the time when I should have been at home was filling up with my attendance at a growing number of union and Labour Party meetings. I was elected as a delegate to the TASS Divisional Council, the regional body of the union representing branches in Bristol, Somerset, Devon and Cornwall (later expanded to include Gloucestershire and Wiltshire). This met at weekends. I was also a member of the political sub-committee of the Divisional Council, which met on weekday evenings to discuss political lobbying and union involvement in Labour Party policymaking. I was a union delegate to Bristol West Labour Party, which also met on weekday evenings at St Barnabas School, St Paul's, and a delegate to the Bristol District Labour Party where activists discussed city council politics. This also met on weekday evenings, as did the Broad Left meetings and my Henleaze Labour Party and union branch meetings. In short, these commitments meant that Eileen and the children were left at home alone far too often and domestic tensions were building. To make matters worse, I had decided to commence studying Open University courses. I thought this might help me make more theoretical sense of my political and trade union work. Little did I know that my studies would eventually lead to a radical change in career. I commenced with the module National Income and Economic Policy. By the end of the year, I had achieved my first distinction but that didn't help matters at home.

Back at the Filton plant we considered various ways of supporting the miners. The South Wales Miners' Federation, known as 'the Fed', had appointed Tony Davies, the NUM secretary of the Merthyr Lodge, as their liaison officer with the Bristol Miners' Support Campaign. We had already met a few times so I invited him to speak at our TASS Bristol No 4 Branch meeting in the early summer of 1984. This was well attended with a generous collection. We also commenced distributing copies of *The Miner Special Issue*, the NUM's journal which gave regular updates on the dispute. Following this I arranged for Tony to speak at a mass meeting of our members on site, where we could hold another collection. Management refused to cooperate, of course, and would not offer a building to house the meeting, so we retaliated by holding it on the steps of the management canteen during their lunch break. Managers had to make their way through the crowd and then climb past Tony who was belting out a speech on a loud hailer.

I indicated earlier that there were two events of importance in 1984. The second was the manual unions' occupation, in late July, of both the naval weapons and commercial aircraft plants at Filton. The context was the changing relationship between management and the unions, brought about by new government marketisation policies. For the aerospace sector, the 1970s were notable for generous 'cost-plus' contracts in defence. These had evolved during the Cold War arms race to support arms manufacturers. Cost-plus meant that companies were paid the full cost of producing a weapons system (often inflated) and an additional allowance for profit. In the commercial aircraft sector, meanwhile, the government paid considerable subsidies to contribute to the cost of developing new aircraft. The Thatcher government commenced reducing these subsidies and, in defence, replaced cost-plus with competitive tendering. This meant that UK defence companies were forced to compete with international contractors, especially in the USA, and thus to cut costs significantly to survive. The impact at the plant level was a tightening of the screw on labour costs.

The disputes at Filton were ostensibly over pay, but the underlying problem was that management was toughening up on work supervision, discipline and sickness as well as pay levels. Disagreements over inter-plant pay parity catalysed the dispute at Commercial Aircraft. At Naval Weapons, a previous pay agreement had included a productivity scheme. When management subsequently announced that plant productivity performance could not support any bonus payments for the shop floor, the leading manual stewards decided that this was the last straw. Whether by management's incompetent design or pure coincidence, the two disputes blew up at exactly the same time. Whilst there was a degree of coordination between the leading stewards at the two plants, which essentially comprised one large sprawling site built around an airfield at Filton, the disputes were fought separately.

STOP PRESS

Preliminary talks with the Coal Board had begun as *The Miner* went to Press.

The union made its position absolutely clear: Threats of closures and redundancies must be withdrawn.

Time was ripe for an expansion of the industry based on the Plan for Coal. More talks are due to be held next week.

Meanwhile Stock Exchange suffered unheard of see-sawing with swings of up to 28.2 per cent.

Strike action by the seamen, planned action by the postmen, continuing action by the teachers and growing discontent in other industries added to the scale of the crisis.

THEY'RE CRACKING

Britain's miners are on the road to a crushing victory.

Despite the most intense campaign to keep the facts from the people — Energy Secretary Peter Walker has even gone to the extraordinary lengths of phoning editors to keep stories out of some papers — the facts are at last getting to people's ears.

The most dramatic news concerns coal stocks. Talk of massive supplies at the stations has been a hoax. In the North as a whole, up to 90 per

By NUM President ARTHUR SCARGILL

cent of coal fired generating capacity has been shut down at certain periods in a panic-stricken attempt to eke out the remaining bits of coal.

Among those to have suffered part or full closures is Eggborough in the North East, Drax, Ferrybridge A and Thorpe Marsh in the North Yorkshire Area and Fiddler's Ferry in Lancashire.

The pattern is becoming clear: Stocks are being stretched to their limits in a crazy gamble which the Prime Minister of this country is taking. Her desperate hope is that she can postpone power cuts.

For she is only too aware that once those cuts begin, she will be exposed to the country as criminally irresponsible.

Nuclear power stations are being run past their maintenance check dates, and oil — now 50 per cent more expensive than coal — is being burnt at an insane rate.

Mrs Thatcher is bleeding this country to death financially in a lunatic bid to maintain her Iron Maiden ego.

The dispute has already cost over £2,200m — twice the amount spent in the Falklands conflict.

But that situation cannot go on: There are some people Mrs Thatcher can't ignore — and their voice has been growing louder over the past few weeks.

I refer to the men of money.

On May 30th, the FT shares index dropped 22.8 points, the second biggest fall on record.

The biggest drop was on March 1st, 1974, the day after the Heath Government fell following our last dispute.

SIGNAL

And is is highly significant that Thatcher, for the first time, has been *forced* to drop her anti-miner hate tone, saying on May 24th that she "earnestly hoped" that talks on the dispute would succeed.

There is no way in which Mrs Thatcher expresses such sentiments unless she is on the run.

And that is exactly what is now beginning to happen.

Already MacGregor — her blue-eyed butcher — has been humiliatingly forced to absent himself from talks with the union, a state of affairs unheard of for the head of a major industry.

His credibility is sub-zero and already questions are being asked of those who appointed him.

It is a clear and effective signal that the miners of Britain will not be trifled with. By anybody.

It now needs to register clearly with MacGregor's political masters and any other would-be MacGregors in the National Coal Board.

A secure and expanding industry with improved conditions is on the horizon, paving the way for the country's industrial regeneration.

All we have to do is keep our nerve and treat the mass media with the contempt it deserves.

Miners, miners' wives, seamen, railmen, dockers, factory and plant workers, white collar workers, print workers, health workers, OAPs, the young, the unemployed, you are all playing a magnificent role in putting hope back into this country.

Our victory will be your victory.

Mounted madmen deliberately trying to trample miners at British Steel's Orgreave plant. Coke is being shifted to Scunthorpe in defiance of an agreement with the Yorkshire NUM. A little known fact is tha Ian MacGregor still remains on the board of British Steel. See pages 4 and 5.

A copy of *The Miner*, the NUM newspaper.
The photo is of the Battle of Orgreave.

Just over 2,000 manual workers were involved at Commercial Aircraft, which at the time was a large design and manufacturing site. At Naval Weapons, the manufacturing areas were smaller, employing around 450 fitters and machinists, organised by the AUEW and TGWU, and another 200 electricians organised by the EETPU. The leading AUEW steward was Mike Harrington, a big guy and someone that you crossed at your peril. When management broke the news about the productivity deal, Mike Harrington, other shop stewards and volunteers moved swiftly overnight to occupy part of the site that contained a portion of Naval Weapons and also the BAe Space Division. The remainder of Naval Weapons was based on the main site that also housed Commercial Aircraft. The AUEW, TGWU and EETPU stewards at Commercial Aircraft organised a complete occupation of that site the same night. Thus, by the end of July, two BAe factories, that in combination employed over 10,000 workers, were occupied by nearly 2,500 manual workers. Once established, different shifts of volunteers took turns to maintain the occupation.

It lasted three weeks. During this time around 7,500 white-collar workers and managers were locked out. The two white-collar unions, AUEW-TASS and APEX representing clerical workers, were not party to the dispute and our involvement was limited to sending motions of support. Initially, we were all sent home but after a week or so management decided to attempt to bring together some of the design teams by renting office space in the city centre. Of course, without access to the site CAD system and other computer technology, much of this was purely cosmetic, and expensive at that. On 8th August, BAe was granted a High Court order for the repossession of both Filton plants. The occupation came to an end when days later the Under Sheriff of Avon, supported by 200 police, forcibly gained control of the site.

This was when the problems started for my union. As soon as the occupation ended, the manual unions placed mass pickets on all entrances to the two sites. Our managers demanded that all staff return to work and our members were looking to us for some guidance. Some of our reps thought that the best solution was to do nothing, to sit back and watch the confusion as some members returned to work while others stayed out. I decided that we needed to hold a mass meeting and ask one of our TASS full-time officials to address the membership. The emotive issue of course, amplified by the miners' strike, was whether we should cross picket lines. I say emotive because the reality of the situation was that we should cross these lines. We were not party to the dispute and in the past the different unions had long established agreements that their factory-gate picket lines were designed to keep out suppliers plus any of their own dissenting members, rather than other non-affected groups. Nevertheless, on this occasion, I was expecting something different from our paid officials. In the event, as Derek Perkins was on holiday, we had Charles Lomas speak to a large mass meeting in the main Filton car park. And he stated in no uncertain terms that we had to go back to work. This caused some dismay for some sections of the membership and a bitter taste for quite some time.

Events took a surprising turn on 23rd August when the 200 Naval Weapons electricians who had not taken part in the main occupation joined the strike and re-occupied that part of the site containing the Space Division and some of Naval Weapons. This lasted for another week. As I knew a good number of the strikers, I visited the new occupation a series of times to see how they were all getting on. Pretty well as far as I could see. There were regular on-site football and cricket matches and games of rounders to keep out the boredom. And plenty of donations of food and alcohol. I invited Charlie Fenwick and Chris Evans, the two leading EETPU stewards, to come to our August TASS branch meeting. In the event Chris turned up to explain the background to the dispute. He also made it very clear that he would have no problem with our members crossing their picket lines, which did calm tempers a bit.

One amusing incident occurred during this second occupation. One site director, Alf Gale, a large man who dressed in a pin-stripe suit and who regularly strolled around the factory smoking Churchillian sized cigars, had parked his holiday caravan on the Space site before it was re-occupied. And he wanted to go on holiday. Eventually he approached the pickets to explain his problem and naturally they all refused to allow him access. He then had a fit of rage and like a mad man began charging at the locked gate with a pair of industrial bolt cutters. After amusing themselves at this entertainment for an hour or so the pickets eventually relented and let him in.

In late September, two months after these disputes began, settlements were reached with a new productivity deal at Naval Weapons and a compromise on pay parity at Commercial Aircraft. But the hostility between the shopfloor and management remained. A few years later a personnel manager told me that one senior steward had threatened to break his legs—and he believed he meant it—if he ever reneged on an agreement again.

1984 ended with some pretty intense discussions at Bristol West Constituency Labour Party meetings, mostly about the miners' strike and specifically with regard to Neil Kinnock's role as Labour leader. Kinnock was elected leader in 1983 following Michael Foot's post-general-election resignation. He presented himself as a left-wing Tribunite and received over 70% of the members' vote. However, he soon started to re-position himself towards the centre and began abandoning policies such as nationalisation of key industries and withdrawal from the EEC (now European Union). He also began attacking left-wing municipal politics and particularly the influence of the Militant Tendency in Liverpool and London. A few months into 1985, he appointed a young media savvy guy called Peter Mandelson, the UK's first 'spin doctor', to modernise the party—a euphemism for moving it very clearly to the right. Kinnock's position on the miners' strike was that he supported the miners themselves, but firmly rejected the NUM's tactics. He detested Arthur Scargill.

With all this going on, I witnessed many animated and at times hostile debates amongst the Bristol West delegates. Often there were close to 100 members present. I was a TASS delegate and I did try to feed in official TASS views which were well on the left, for example, on nationalisation, the EEC and the miners' strike. Some of the key characters on the left at Bristol West meetings were Keith Elliot, Don McLaren (the chair) and Hedley Bashforth. Some were very articulate academics who I did enjoy listening to, but I often felt nervous about standing up to speak for fear of making a fool of myself. Over the years this nervousness wore off and I eventually became more outspoken at these meetings. The small London-based Trotskyist group, Socialist Action (associated with support for Ken Livingstone and the GLC), was well represented. As far as I can remember there were only a couple of Militant Tendency supporters, one of whom was a very strange character who turned up each month dressed only in a shirt and a large leather thong. Every month motions attacking various Kinnock positions were debated and I invariably supported them. They were mostly passed but inevitably ignored by the leadership. In those days there were no right wingers at these meetings; the pro-Kinnock group was more centre-left, people like Doug Naysmith (who eventually became an MP), Mary Georghiou (obsessed with proportional representation), Nigel Curry (a sociology schoolteacher who eventually joined the Conservative Party) and Judy Patterson and Pat McLaren (local councillors). We had some disagreements, but I mostly got on well with them; indeed, a good number were close neighbours in Henleaze and Redland. After each Bristol West meeting many of us would walk around the corner from St Barnabas School to the Star and Garter pub. This was one of the great meeting places for the Afro-Caribbean community in St Pauls. There were two bars. One was often packed with locals playing dominos noisily; the other, where we headed, was notable for the reggae music played by a local white DJ who looked incongruously like a stuffy accountant. He was DJ Derek, soon to become a Bristol legend.

1985 Despair, the Annual Conference and the Aerospace Lobbies

I had my name down to take the food collection over to Penrhiwceiber on 3rd March 1985. Eileen was working so I decided to bring the kids, Jess and Detta, now aged five and four. We were accompanied by Phil Harrison, a good friend and TASS negotiating committee colleague, and his partner Dawn. As it turned out, this was not a felicitous choice of date. It was the day the strike was called off and the atmosphere that greeted us on a cold grey day was predictably bleak. A French film company was making a documentary on the strike that day, so to get out of their way a miner volunteered to take the girls and me around the pit head and the miners' lodge. Thankfully we were not allowed underground or even inside the pit cage. It's strange how you remember small things. When we were in the lodge I was talking to a couple of miners when Detta got off my lap, walked up to an ashtray on the table in front of us and blew the lot over the miners. Luckily, they were very amused.

As far as I was concerned the strike was about two core issues. First, defeating the government and thus strengthening the morale of the British trade union movement at a time when union rights were under relentless attack. In this respect, following the outcome of the strike, I despaired at the number of times I was stopped by my members in corridors along the No1 Drawing Office to be told that if the miners can't win then nobody can. Second, defending the many working-class mining communities that faced oblivion in the event of a defeat. On this point, an end note on the fate of Penrhiwceiber is that the pit was closed in October 1985. In 2019, Penrhiwceiber was named as the council ward

Detta and Jess at the Penrhiwceiber pit, 3rd March 1985.

Ken Gill and Arthur Scargill at the 1985
TASS Annual Representative Council Conference.

with the highest rate of child poverty in Wales, at 49%. In other words, every other child is living in poverty.[9]

I'm pretty sure that the first time I heard Arthur Scargill speak was at my first TASS Annual Representative Council Conference (the union's annual conference) held at Bournemouth in June 1985. He gave the guest keynote speech which mixed humour with defiance and of course received a big ovation. The conference in those days, before the big mergers, was relatively small, typically under 200 delegates. These were elected from district conferences to which delegates were elected from the divisional councils; branches nominated delegates to the latter. The point to remember is that of the branch union activists who wished to get involved with the work of the union outside of the workplace, the vast majority were Broad Left supporters.

I attended all seven annual conferences from 1985 to 1991. I moved motions at each of these on subjects ranging from discrimination at work, to defence procurement, to arms conversion, to the threat of the rise of the so-called periphery workforce (sub-contract labour, agency labour, the self-employed, etc). All conference motions that received Broad Left support were carried. Any that did not receive such support inevitably failed (at least until the end of the decade when TASS merged with ASTMS). My first conference speech was to move a motion attacking Thatcher's anti-union law and was a bit nerve wracking. I walked up to the podium where there were fixed three light bulbs which gave you a maximum of five minutes. Green indicating that you start speaking, amber indicating you have a minute left, and red when you had to stop or the conference chair would cut you out. I practiced my speech a few times beforehand and I managed to time it perfectly. As a newcomer I also received a big round of applause. So I was happy with that.

This 1985 conference is one I remember clearly for a number of reasons, not due to Scargill's appearance but rather the behaviour of those delegates who were Communist Party members. I was sitting in the main lobby of the Bournemouth hotel hosting the conference, enjoying a drink whilst waiting for the main Broad Left meeting that always took place on the evening before conference business commenced. The meeting was to discuss how we should vote on certain motions and elections. I was chatting with Ron Warren, my union counterpart at Rolls Royce Bristol. Ron guided me though this first conference and he became a good colleague. Suddenly, the lobby, which was pretty full,

9 https://www.bbc.co.uk/news/uk-wales-48259327, Child Poverty: Wales is the only UK country to see an increase, accessed 4 December 2020.

I'm at the podium moving my first motion at the 1985 TASS Conference.

emptied, leaving just a few of us behind. I said to Ron, "shouldn't we go?". He laughed and explained that was not our meeting but a meeting of the Communist Party delegates who would decide in advance how the Broad Left meeting should proceed.

It was from this point onwards that I joined up with Ron and a few others from the South West who were either Labour Party outsiders or plain non-party outsiders. The likes of Jim Black, Eric Marks and Dave Giles, all from the Westland plants, and in later years, delegates from Dowty in Gloucester and the Rover plant in Swindon. Across the country there were others, for instance, groups of Trotskyist stewards at the Rolls Royce plant in Coventry. It was never the case that the communist delegates shunned us, and my FTO Derek Perkins was always very friendly at these events, but tensions did exist, and we resented the way in which they assumed that we should know our place.

One egregious example of this was the case of Dave Kitson. He was originally a draughtsman in the UK aerospace industry and a keen TASS activist. He was also a member of the Communist Party, but no Stalinist. In 1959, Kitson married Norma Cranko, a South African Communist Party activist and moved there just months before the Sharpeville massacre. He then joined up with uMkhonto we Sizwe, the ANC's armed wing, and became involved with its sabotage campaign. He was eventually arrested and sentenced to 20 years in prison. When he had served his term, he moved back to London in the early 1980s, teamed up again with Norma and they remarried, having divorced while he was imprisoned. Norma had founded the City of London Anti-Apartheid Group, notable for staging non-stop protests outside South Africa's embassy in Trafalgar Square. The cautious leadership of the UK's Anti-Apartheid Movement was not happy with this confrontational style to the extent that eventually the ANC and London cell of the South African Communist Party told Kitson to denounce his wife. He refused. This is where the TASS union came in. Kitson had been promised a lectureship at Ruskin College but this was withdrawn following the intervention of TASS, of Ken Gill in fact. This decision generated a good deal of anger within the non-CP membership of the Broad Left. I was told that it blew up at the annual conference in 1984, and it did so again in 1985. All attempts from the floor to overturn the decision were countered by interventions from some of the Communist Party delegates and rejected by the leadership on the main platform. Some of us from the South West were pretty angry about this.

Overall, 1985 was not an eventful year on the industrial relations front at Filton. We followed up the manual workers' pay dispute with one of our own and managed to implement a short-lived overtime ban in the spring, along with a drawing office sectional strike that lasted just a few days. But having just recovered from the 1984 occupations, management had no wish to test our resolve and offered a pay increase slightly in excess of the inflation rate along with a £150 consolidated bonus payment. This was accepted by the members despite our recommendation to reject. Pay grievances were nevertheless building up on the office floor.

Nationally, the union finally broke away from the AUEW, following years of acrimony between Ken Gill and the AUEW leadership. This had little impact on relations between the manual and non-manual sections at most factories, including Filton. In our case, although we would regularly talk to some of the leading stewards, the manual workforce was rarely interested in the idea of joint action with the non-manuals who they saw as weakening their own collective power. Another difference, which corresponded with the divisions at the top of the union, was that many leading TASS activists were far to the left of the manual stewards who, despite their militancy, and of course with one or two exceptions, often appeared to us as either Labour moderates or uninterested in politics.

I did become involved in two union initiatives aimed at supporting jobs in the industry. The first was the TASS 'Keep Aerospace Flying' campaign organised by our national officer Chris Darke. The idea, as put by Ken Gill, was that as manufacturing is crucial to Britain's future and the aerospace industry is the epitome of high technology then governments must halt the steady loss of jobs and skills in the sector. Lobbies of Tory MPs and senior Labour figures were organised. In July, I travelled to London with groups of senior stewards from BAe, Rolls Royce, Westland Helicopters, Dowty Aerospace and Smiths Industries to speak to MPs and then handed a large postcard and petition to Number 10 Downing Street. The postcard message read,

> Dear Prime Minister: The South West aerospace industry can beat the French, the Germans, the Americans, the Japanese, and any others for design, quality and efficiency. But we cannot beat the British government as well. Please support us. We deserve it.[10]

And did she? Fat chance of that but it wasn't for the lack of trying—it was the first of many lobbies I took part in.

The other initiative was the recently formed South West-based Better Future for Defence Jobs Committee (BFDJC), which I joined. Named after a TGWU booklet, the committee aimed to discuss the prospects for arms conversion in the region and to support any local rank-and-file initiatives that might emerge. Arms conversion means converting factories that produce weapons of war to producing socially useful products. The idea was based on the 1970s campaign led by TASS member Mike Cooley and others at Lucas Aerospace to avoid workforce redundancies by converting production. The BFDJC had official and lay representatives from different defence sector unions (though, in truth, dominated by TASS) along with the TUC Regional Secretary Phil Gregory and a Bristol University academic, John Lovering. I became an active and vocal supporter of this committee, an involvement that would greatly help the launch of a conversion campaign at my own plant three years later.

10 TASS News and Journal, July/August 1985.

Five Broad Left members at 10 Downing Street: Peter Luck, Ron Warren, me, Dave Giles and Rose Keeping.

1986: The Blue Book and a miscellany of problems

In early January 1986, I drew up a pay claim based on the Blue Book data provided to all BAe negotiating teams by Chris Darke. As indicated earlier, the Blue Book arose out of a negotiating policy discussion in 1984 at the TASS National Aerospace Committee. It provided excellent in-depth analysis of BAe accounts and other financial indicators. I was very pleased with my draft claim. It dissected the company's recently-announced half-year financial performance (profits up 21%; sales up 22%; earnings per share up 17%; and dividends up 10.5%), important because each year management habitually claimed the company was in financial difficulties a couple of months ahead of pay negotiations. The claim noted the rate of inflation and changes in direct and indirect taxation since 1979 resulting in a drop in living standards and large increases in housing mortgage costs consequent upon the rise in interest rates. Our claim was for a flat-rate increase of £1,000 per annum to address the growing gap between our lowest and highest paid members.[11]

---

11 TASS Bristol No 4 Branch Newsletter, 1986 Annual Wage Claim, 1985.

Later that month our negotiating committee met Ernie Peck and his negotiating team to present our claim. The tradition was that the TASS negotiating committee chair would formally present the claim, helped by the secretary, and then the rest of the committee had their pennyworth. The chair of our committee was still Alan Stevens, a design engineer and a somewhat loquacious character who enjoyed plentiful pints of beer at lunchtime. When we had all sat down for the afternoon negotiating session, Alan proceeded to present our claim using the Blue Book rather than my notes. As his presentation developed, I became somewhat confused because I did not recognise the figures he was using. When he had finished, I decided not to add anything and invited Ernie Peck to respond for the company. We then spent a good couple of hours arguing about the contrast between the company's pleas of poverty and the Blue Book data. Peck argued that although our data were accurate, they nevertheless, like all published company finance reports, concealed a more complex and challenging picture. Eventually we agreed to adjourn until the following day when the company would make a formal offer. As we left the building, I asked Alan to hand me his Blue Book. I was horrified to find that he had brought the previous year's edition based on the company's 1985 financial performance. In the end the committee fell about laughing at this. We knew of course that it didn't matter what figures we were armed with. Ernie Peck's response would always be formed by head office diktat—the process of plant negotiation was only ever a charade.

The following day, Peck responded with an offer of a general increase of 4.25% plus £50 for those on a salary of less than £10,000 and a straight increase of 4.75% for those earning £10,000 or more. The offer was flatly rejected by the negotiating committee and this was endorsed by a subsequent mass meeting of members. In the middle of February, Peck returned with the same basic offer but with an additional element. A productivity incentive scheme would potentially pay £100 in July and another £100 in December most of which would be consolidated. We again rejected this, but we believed the membership might eventually accept it.

Meanwhile other TASS negotiating teams around the country were settling on similar terms and this was undermining our opposition. At the same time some senior managers at our Filton plant began attacking the TASS organisation by holding departmental meetings of staff where they claimed that Bristol trade unions were more militant than elsewhere, that local industrialists regarded Bristol as a 'militant city', and that TASS at Filton had been taken over by communist militants who did not represent their members' views. A friend of mine attended one of these meetings and informed me that my name was mentioned. Some managers even began interviewing members who they believed voted the 'wrong way' at mass meetings. Although these were dirty tricks, I'm happy to concede that there was an element of truth in what they were saying, though none of us were communists. With the exception of Alan Stevens and one or two others, the TASS union reps on the JOC were relatively new to activism, relatively young and more militant in outlook. Four of the six negotiating committee reps were Broad Left members as were some of the JOC and branch officials. The complexion of our workplace union activists had changed radically compared to when I joined in 1979.

In the event, although the negotiating committee recommended rejection, the membership did, reluctantly, accept the offer in April. In our routine post-mortem discussion at the next branch meeting, we predicted that we were heading for a big dispute in 1987.

Apart from occasional individual grievances and disciplinary cases, we became involved in negotiations on a number of important issues not directly connected to pay. The first, in July 1986, was a management proposal to replace the intake of 20 four-year technician apprenticeships with two-year Youth Training Scheme (YTS) technical traineeships. The Thatcher government introduced the YTS ostensibly in response to high levels of youth unemployment and a severe decline in traditional apprenticeships. Of course, the reason for both was the government's decimation of manufacturing industry. The reality of many YTS schemes was that high quality training would be replaced by a system of low-quality education and cheap labour. Accordingly, we flatly rejected the company's submission. Management then came back to us with a new proposal. They agreed that the quality and structure of the training would remain unchanged and that after two years the trainees would revert to conventional third- and fourth-year apprenticeships. Also, the pay and conditions of the YTS trainees would be the same as for apprenticeships. We again firmly rejected this on the basis that all the company was doing was receiving government finance to contribute towards its pre-existing training programmes. In other words, we told them it was a scam. After a series of further meetings, we finally persuaded management to use the money to increase the number of traineeships/apprenticeships to 25. In addition, Alan Stevens and I would have an input into the trainees' induction course, allowing us to teach the youngsters about the role of trade unions. Which we did. I guess it's a small example from many of the role of trade unions in bringing about positive change at the workplace of a type that is rarely reported by the media.

The mid-1980s was also a period when some of the larger employers began attempting to improve their image by introducing equal opportunities policies. British Aerospace was one of these. In April 1986, management announced to the workforce that it was to introduce such a policy. Comically, the policy in its entirety was a statement that "management will treat all job applicants and employees equally, irrespective of sex, marital status, race, colour, nationality, or ethnic or national origin". We met management to tell them that national codes of practice call for consultation and negotiation with trade unions on such matters. Moreover, that we were not interested in glib policy statements. Instead, we would submit an authentic equal opportunity policy that established how principles would be put into practice. In response, management agreed to research their personnel records and provide data on numbers of female staff and managers and ethnic minority staff and managers. The results provided only a crude breakdown of the figures, but they were still shocking. I remember them well as I used them in later years as a university lecturer. There were approximately 300 female staff out of a workforce of 4,700 and most of these were lower paid clerical workers. Just two women were managers out of a total of over 600! The figures for ethnic minorities were even worse. They comprised less than one percent of the workforce with just one junior manager. This confirmed to us what we already knew, that BAe was overwhelmingly white and male and it needed to change. And so began a long, painful, drawn out negotiating process that lasted a full five years. I shall come back to it eventually.

Another routine activity was the negotiation, or renegotiation, of grading schemes. This could be a complicated affair because there was no site-wide scheme. Instead, a plethora of schemes operated in different departments, covering different types of jobs. A good deal of effort had to be expended to ensure that job roles and skills were consistently defined and that pay differentials were fair. One persistent headache for us was management's differentiation between what they termed 'job-based' and 'career-based' staff. Job-based staff could progress their careers (and salary) only by changing jobs with fixed grades. That is by applying for vacancies in their department or other departments. Career-based staff might remain in the same basic job over time but still move through their grades. On occasion, some might also receive generous 'market adjusted' salary increases in addition to any annual pay increase or merit award. Why this irrational distinction? The real reason was that career-based staff were mostly graduate engineers and as such their managers felt that trade union membership was inappropriate. Certainly, the idea that these engineers could take industrial action was anathema. Consequently, we never had formal union recognition in the career-based areas, although the company turned a blind eye to the fact that four career-based representatives sat on our TASS JOC and two were members of the negotiating committee. Moreover, any pay or other agreement we negotiated was applied to these staff. Indeed, Ernie Peck seemed happy for us to negotiate on their behalf if only on an unofficial basis.

Despite these concessions, the distinction worked for management in a classic 'divide and rule' sense. Out of a total membership of 900 in 1986, around 600 were in job-based departments, each with high membership densities, whilst only around 200 graduate engineers were members out of a possible 1,000 in the career-based departments. And these 200 required tough skins. Some managers regularly threatened them with damage to their careers if they continued membership or, worse still, took part in industrial action. Equally, when we did take such action, a disproportionate number of resignations would come from career-based departments. For our TASS workplace organisation this was a real problem. Our occasional claims for union recognition were consistently rebuffed by the company. So, in November 1986, we launched a campaign to win a grading scheme to cover all career-based engineers. Management had already admitted to us that the existing career-based grade categories of engineer, higher engineer, senior engineer and principal engineer carried no job descriptions or agreed ways of progressing from grade to grade. The grades had no minimum or maximum salaries and the method of allocating individuals to grades was purely at management's discretion.

Initially, the campaign comprised recruitment drives which succeeded in a limited sense, though not sufficient to win recognition. We then circulated staff surveys designed to highlight the inequities of the current system and to embarrass the company. The results of one such survey exposed many salary discrepancies and systematic discrimination against older engineers, for example, 25-year-old engineers in the lowest grade receiving higher salaries than older engineers in the highest grade. We put together a draft grading scheme that contained more grades, clear skill and qualification requirements, supervisory criteria and suggested salary bands. Over the following years the company sat down to negotiate informally with us, but they could never concede that our input was officially recognised. In the event, three years later, in November 1989, the company did indeed introduce a career-based grading scheme. This included nine new grades, qualification criteria, years of experience, supervisory experience, and salary bands with minimum salaries. We didn't accept the scheme because movement through the grades remained entirely at management's discretion. Nevertheless, most of our demands were included.

In the late summer of 1986, the site management announced that the first £100 of the incentive scheme which had been agreed when we had settled our pay claim a few months earlier would not now be paid. The reasons they gave were that, first, insufficient new orders were coming in and, second, the company had decided to pay £16 million worth of outstanding bills. We were enraged by this, as were our members. We knew that our finance director had issued instructions earlier in the year that bills be paid as late as possible. Thus, management knew the bills had to be paid in June at the time the incentive scheme was designed, and we consequently argued that they had intentionally sabotaged the scheme. The TASS negotiating committee met management and suggested staff be paid in full and management be paid nothing, a fair reflection of their ability. And then we walked out. We told our members that the 1987 claim would take full cognisance of this double dealing.

During the autumn, again with the help of the Blue Book (the correct year this time), I drew up a new pay claim. This was for a 10% rise or £900 pa whichever was the greater. As in 1986 the claim was based on arguments that highlighted big increases in the company's pre-tax profits, on windfall profits from the sale of land at the recently closed Weybridge site, on increased share dividends, and on increased orders across all divisions. Although the RPI stood at 3% at the end of 1986, we argued that the rate of inflation on mortgage interest rates stood at over 18%. We also put into play two additional factors. The company accounts showed that senior management pay had risen by nearly 9% over the year and this was on top of management profit-share schemes, free company cars and other perks. The second factor was the outcome of the manual unions' productivity scheme agreed at the end of their occupation and strike in 1984. The scheme was due to terminate in December 1986 and the unions had agreed with management that £700 per year would be consolidated into their wages. Of course, we congratulated the manual unions on this settlement but argued that the pay differential between a shop-floor worker and an engineer had narrowed dramatically. And there was the failure of our staff incentive scheme which in the event paid just £96 over the whole year.[12]

We disseminated these details and much more to the membership. The negotiating committee sat down with Ernie Peck and other industrial managers at the end of November to receive the company's initial reply. As with most years their rationale was that the company accounts rarely reflected the health of the organisation. For example, although financial analysts always used pre-tax profits as an accurate indicator of company profitability, this year our management preferred to use the post-tax figure which was lower. Also, while we had argued that the Weybridge site closure would generate windfall profits, management replied that the closure appeared as an extraordinary cost item of £44 million in the accounts, to pay for redundancies. We pointed out that every newspaper in the country had highlighted the fact that BAe owned 132 acres of development land at Weybridge worth £1 million per acre and rising. I could go on. During my time at BAe, I spent many, many hours arguing intensely with management about such figures but things always boiled down to the same basic issue—for us and for management—were we prepared to do anything about it? When management tabled their initial derisory offer of 3%, we believed that this year we were heading for a major dispute.

Just before the Christmas break, management improved the offer to 3.5% which we flatly rejected. Going back through all the membership newsletters I wrote in this period, I noted that they were packed with data of the type our members liked. These were used for propaganda purposes, but they worked. For instance, detailed analysis of offers made at other BAe sites, some of which were superior to ours, analysis of UK settlements across the engineering sector—only the better ones of course—and much material on recent directors' pay rises, including that of our own, Sir Austin Pearce, who received a 21% increase.

12 TASS Bristol No 4 Branch Newsletter, 1987 Pay Claim, October 1986.

1987: A pay strike at last

Following a number of additional meetings with management in January 1987, during which they changed tack in emphasising that the site was losing orders and was in trouble, the TASS Joint Office Committee voted unanimously to register a 'failure to agree'. This triggered a Works Conference with the Engineering Employers Federation, the final stage in the avoidance of the disputes procedure. As was the norm, the offer did not improve at this conference. We then arranged a mass meeting on 23rd February, where we prepared to hold a strike ballot.

Our plan of attack was shaped by the knowledge that, unlike for the manuals, indefinite strikes hurt our members more than the company, at least in the short term. Our proposal was therefore to hold either half-day or whole-day strikes each week, backed up by regular sectional strikes in those departments that might hurt the company most. In addition, we would operate a work-to-rule and go-slow.

The Tory Government's Trade Union Act 1984 had made secret ballots in advance of industrial action compulsory. At that stage it did not state clearly that postal ballots should be adopted, though that was the expectation. I drafted a fairly simple ballot form, which asked members whether or not they were prepared to take strike action and action short of a strike to further the TASS pay claim. I suggested to the negotiating committee that, because the union opposed this legislation, we should not put ourselves out to fully comply with it. At the mass meeting, held in a packed canteen, we gave a full report of negotiations and explained why we were recommending rejection of the company offer and why our only option on this occasion was to take industrial action. We then took a show of hands to see if the membership also rejected the offer, which they did overwhelmingly. Following this, our JOC reps circulated the ballot forms. When ready we took a second show of hands on the question of taking strike action, asking members to hold their completed ballot forms in the air. Finally, we collected the forms and counted the votes. The result was strong support for striking, in the region of 70% of the membership, and close to 100% for action short of a strike. At these mass meetings the company always had one or two spies present, quietly monitoring proceedings. About a month after the meeting, Derek Perkins rang me to say he had received a letter from the EEF explaining that they were in the process of taking legal action against the union for our failure to comply with the Trade Union

Act and that my name was cited as the person responsible for this. We agreed this was a scare tactic aimed at forcing us to re-ballot. We decided to ignore the letter.

We started the action on my birthday, Friday 27th February, with a half day strike. We decided that the weekly strikes would always be on a Friday so as to give the members a long weekend. In effect these strikes constituted the drumbeat of our action, never called off, always on a Friday and thus leaving little room for confusion. They lasted until the first week of July. The half day strikes were preceded by open air mass meetings to report any news and to keep up morale.

By the first week of March, we had been joined in the dispute by the clerical union APEX and both manual unions, the AUEW and EETPU, although at that stage they were not taking any industrial action. On Friday 13th March, a mass meeting of TASS members voted overwhelmingly to maintain the weekly strikes and commence further disruptive action. The following Tuesday our illustrators in the Technical Publications Department staged a one-hour walkout. On Wednesday members in the Estimating, Configuration and Standards Departments staged a two-hour walkout, while the whole of the Drawing Office plus the Calibration and Maintenance Department walked out for the entire afternoon. On Thursday, computer operators, data controllers and programmers staged another half day strike. On Friday morning the negotiating committee joined Test and Planning engineers in occupying the paint shop behind the main MPS production plant. We succeeded in halting production for the day. All TASS members staged the usual half-day strike in the afternoon. The same pattern of disruptive action took place the following week and this time, for the sectional strikes, we were joined by APEX and the shop-floor unions.

Management refused to talk to us until the last week of March, when, following company practice across all BAe sites, they presented the final financial results for 1986 to all site unions. These showed declines in profits at the Commercial Aircraft and Military Aircraft Divisions—where the unions had been offered pay rises in excess of our 3.5%—and significant increases in profit at Naval Weapons Division. This was cause for some comical retorts on our side. But it was this type of information that helped us to win the propaganda war that was developing and, of course, it was immediately fed back to the members. I produced posters for our notice boards with the text,

On 5th April, the Sunday Times carried an article on the success of BAe. It showed how between 1981 and 1986 employment had fallen by 4,300 whilst turnover per employee was up 133%, profit per employee was up 246% and earnings per share had risen 60%. AND ALL WE GET IS 3.5%. BAe CAN PAY![13]

"BAe Can Pay!" had become our slogan, appearing on placards, posters and newsletters plastered all over the site. In addition, for the first time, we commenced using the media to publicise our cause. I began drafting press releases aimed mostly at the local media and as a result I was interviewed by HTV for a local television bulletin along with *BBC Radio Bristol* and *Great Western Radio*. Favourable reports appeared in the *Financial Times*, the *Bristol Evening Post* and *Western Daily Press*. These interviews and newspaper reports became a regular feature of the dispute and we knew that management hated the coverage since BAe has always been a secretive company obsessed with its public image.

At certain points we attempted to explore ways and means of bettering the company offer but management showed no interest in this. For instance, at the end of March, one month into the dispute, we met management to table three proposals:

1. a consolidation of lump sums from previous bonus systems amounting to around 1% of salary;
2. additional pay increases in our various grading schemes, thus allowing management to hide the true increases paid from the headline settlement;
3. because our members were clearly supporting the Friday strikes we suggested the adoption of a flexitime system allowing staff to go home Friday lunchtimes on a permanent basis.

In the first week of April, we met the new managing director of the BAe Dynamics Group, of which our Naval Weapons Division formed a part, Peter Brighton, who was based at the Stevenage Divisional HQ. He defended the 3.5% pay offer, saying that wage settlements this year and in future years had to be reduced to offset the damaging repercussions of the MOD's drive to cut costs, in particular the new competitive tendering policy. Our reply was that bigger wage increases were going

13 TASS Bristol No 4 Branch Newsletter, 6 April 1987.

to the main production centres such as Warton and Stevenage, whereas the equally important design centres such as Filton were left to take the brunt of the cost cuts. We demanded that he return to BAe HQ at the Strand to request more money. He refused point blank. We told him that, in that case, we'd travel to London ourselves and speak to his bosses directly.

We then continued the disruptive action. In the week we met Peter Brighton, Technical Publications staff took half-day strikes on the Wednesday and Thursday afternoons, and they were joined with walkouts by career-based members in Electronics Technology, along with the Works Engineers and the Procedures Secretariat. Some of these actions were, however, generating some doubts among the less committed union members. We did gain some new members, but some resigned their membership. A small minority of members also scabbed. I caused a bit of an uproar in the main No 1 Drawing Office when I produced posters for all the union noticeboards listing their names. As tensions rose, enraged managers went from board to board tearing them down.

Our next little piece of action was designed primarily to gain more media coverage. On Friday 10th April, before walking out for the weekly strike, we organised a short march around the site and then along Southmead Road to the BAWA Leisure Centre, where company directors were entertaining some visitors. We had a very good turnout with banners, placards and plenty of chanting. The one snag was that the BBC and HTV camera crews and their interviewers arrived at the wrong gate and by the time they realised their mistake they were diverted to a major traffic accident on the M5. Nevertheless, we did get coverage the following morning on breakfast TV and on local radio and the press. We also enjoyed ourselves, surrounding the BAWA club and entertaining the directors and visitors hiding inside.

That same week, the Advisory, Conciliation and Arbitration Service (ACAS) contacted Derek Perkins and offered its facilities in an attempt to settle the dispute. We accepted this offer, but management was not interested. They seemed intent on rigidly sticking to the current offer and perhaps on breaking our union organisation too. On our side, we remained fairly flexible in attempting to find a solution to the impasse, but we were also becoming quite innovative in exploring different forms of action. The next of these was the lobby of company directors at BAe's headquarters in the Strand, London. On Friday 24th April, as most

Marching along Southmead Road, Bristol, 10th April 1987.

members took part in the weekly strike, two coach loads of TASS and APEX members travelled to London early in the morning and spent the day forming a picket line around the entrance of the building, handing out leaflets and chanting "BAe Can Pay!" This was another event that gained media interest, though we didn't detect the same emanating from inside the building.

On 18th April, Eddie Shah's Today newspaper ran an article on BAe's 10th anniversary celebrations, quoting an executive as saying,

> We could have chosen any number of themes to mark our anniversary—from Harrier to our design of the first British spaceplane. But we decided that the workforce were our best resource. No matter what the accountants say, people are the bottom line.[14]

We took great delight in parodying this crass human resource management speak. Then, in the first week of May, the release of the full BAe Annual Report for 1986 provided plenty of further ammunition. The salary of the Chairman, Sir Austin Pearce, rose by 19% and that of

14 *Today*, 18 April 1987.

the Chief Executive, Sir Raymond Lygo, by 18%. The salary bill for BAe's top executives increased by 149% while the number of its highest paid executives more than doubled.

Early May also marked the beginning of weekly one-day strikes, each one announced at short notice by the JOC. However, these continued for just two weeks. At a mass meeting on 13th May, our members voted overwhelmingly to continue the dispute which gave us immense encouragement, given our growing worries about management's dogmatic refusal to enter into any meaningful negotiation. The meeting also agreed to step up our actions. The Friday afternoon strikes would continue but key sections of the membership would also be withdrawn for a series of one-week strikes on full pay, funded by a levy and TASS strike pay. Immediately, an important section of draughtsmen in the No1 Drawing Office went on strike. In addition, we also gave notice that all design office sub-contractors be given 30 days' notice of a ban and that in the meantime sub-contractors take 'like for like' action with our members. This was made possible by a longstanding and wide-ranging union agreement between TASS and the Federation of Engineering Design Companies which allowed our members to control the substitution of sub-contracted engineers for our members' labour. It would not be long before the Tories made such agreements illegal.

From its beginning I remained fully committed to winning the dispute and was totally energised by the experience. But it was exhausting. Alan Stevens, the chair of the Negotiating Committee, had retired before the dispute commenced and he was replaced by Richard Clatworthy, a test engineer and Broad Left supporter who I got on with very well. The dispute was the property of the Joint Office Committee, but Richard and I were the two full-time senior reps responsible for running it. My workload was not helped when, at the beginning of the year I was elected as TASS Divisional Council Secretary, a role similar to a branch secretary but much larger in scope and content. At home, Eileen had become resigned to my ever-growing involvement, but she was also increasingly resentful at my regular absences from the home as the expanding number of union and Labour Party meetings took their toll. And then there was the continuing Open University work—I was studying sociology courses by now. At this point I gave up my position as Secretary of TASS Bristol No 4 Branch and we elected a young woman named Kathy Eastwood as a replacement. Kathy was a great activist. She had joined BAe two years earlier as a social science graduate. I introduced her to the Broad Left, and she became another committed member as well as a Labour Party activist.

The other site unions remained in the dispute. Indeed, by May, APEX had begun staging similar weekly strikes and sectional withdrawals to ours. The manual unions maintained their sporadic sectional walkouts. As the month drew to an end, most BAe divisions and sites had settled their pay claims and nearly all had been awarded increases in excess of our offer, which had not changed since February. The weekly half-day strikes continued, and our computer operators followed the draughtsmen by holding a one-week sectional strike.

Things really started to heat up in the middle of June. Early one morning I was woken by a phone call from Richard Clatworthy. He informed me that some members from his Test Department and the Calibration and Maintenance Department had entered the main MPS production building and initiated an occupation. MPS was a huge, cavernous structure, housing most of the site's production activity along with large departments of test engineers, production planners, production engineers and administrators. One of our negotiating committee members, Phil Harrison, along with Mike Parker (an SWP activist), Tim Kenneally and a few others had, in the middle of the night, walked into the building's main entrance which was staffed by a team of company security policemen. When they announced that it was a union occupation, the policemen, all TGWU members, allowed them to take over.

I arranged to meet Richard at the building entrance as soon as we could get there. Phil and Mike were sat at the security desks and after a hurried meeting we started to get volunteers to come over and maintain the occupation, enough to close down all production activity for the next 24 hours. Richard and I were not bothered that these guys had gone behind our backs and, in some respects, we were expecting such a thing to happen. Members like Phil Harrison and Tim Kenneally came from the Test Department which was notable for its workforce that often adopted a wicked sense of humour and mischievous behaviour to subvert and counter management control.[15] For instance, on the night of the break-in, Tim Kenneally had found his manager's suit hanging in a storage cabinet. His manager was Dick Millard, but he was known as Duck Mallard. Tim put the suit on and spent half the night prancing

---

15 A number of sociologists have published on this subject. See for example: P Taylor and P Bain, '"Subterranean Worksick Blues": Humour as Subversion in Two Call Centres', Organization Studies, Vol.24, Issue 9, November 2003.

around in it. Another example was the creation of an alternative magazine named Hip Shape, a parody of the company site magazine, Ship Shape. This was again the work of Tim. The company's Ship Shape contained information about product news, site developments and local interest stories involving employees and managers. In Tim's very amusing version, amongst the Viz-style comic humour were printed rumours about some managers' marital infidelities and other misdemeanours. Despite considerable effort, management never found out who was responsible.

All in all, we were pleased with this occupation because management were clearly rattled. I have no knowledge of any other case of an occupation by white-collar staff closing down a site's production, even for 24 hours. Midway through the morning, Richard and I received an urgent call to report to Ernie Peck's office. When we arrived, Peck was absolutely livid. He warned us that those responsible for the occupation, including Richard and me, could face disciplinary action. We just smiled and returned to the occupied MPS building, knowing that the strength of membership feeling behind our continuing actions kept us safe.

The Friday afternoon strikes continued until the end of the month, and then it was over. During the final week of June, we had sat down for intensive talks with management and agreed a package of changes that could be put to the membership. On 2nd July, a mass meeting accepted it.

Anyone reading this might assume that we failed miserably. The 3.5% general award remained unchanged. There was an additional sum of £75, of which just £50 would be consolidated. In other words, for an average job-based salary of £10,000 we gained an extra 0.5%. However, management also conceded that a flexitime system would be introduced by October 1988, with negotiations commencing immediately. The system would allow staff to take off one day per month and would include arrangements for an end to the working week on Friday lunchtimes. As I indicated earlier, at the request of our members we had raised the idea of flexitime with management a number of times over the years but had always been met with a brick wall of denial. In truth, flexitime systems were regarded as impractical in manufacturing industry and were virtually unheard of. Certainly, none existed in the aerospace sector, so this was a major concession and a popular one. In the weeks that followed I and my negotiating committee colleagues were met with many smiles and 'well dones' around the site. We did welcome this development but, to be honest, we knew that the fight with management was over money, which we didn't get.

One day in the autumn of 1987, Alf Gale, the site director responsible for production, walked into No1 Drawing Office, puffing on a big cigar as usual and with a wooden soap box in his hands. Once the departmental managers had rounded up their staff for an Alf Gale mass meeting, he jumped on the box and announced, "Lads, we're going to become Japanised". He proceeded to outline the company's plan to introduce quality circles under a scheme titled P3E. In typical lean management-speak this stood for 'People, Productivity and Performance = Efficiency'. My own union, TASS, already had very clear policies that rejected Japanese management techniques. Ken Gill had stated publicly that these were alien practices aimed at squeezing more work and profit out of an overworked workforce. Quality circles were an aspect of this and, at face value, quite harmless. However, the practice of getting workers to meet up in teams to discuss ways of improving work efficiency in reality meant discussing methods of intensifying their workloads. In other words, self-exploitation in the service of profit.

Our negotiating committee and some JOC reps were then called to a meeting with the other site unions to receive a presentation from Alf Gale, Ernie Peck and a team of production and design managers. Although nationally the AUEW and EETPU were courting Japanese employers, this did not necessarily translate into support from the rank and file. When all the managers had completed their turn, the AUEW convenor Mike Harrington stood up and said, "you're really asking us to work harder for this, so are you going to pay us more?" When Alf Gale replied "Well…no, it's not about money", the complete AUEW/EETPU group of around twenty shop stewards just stood up and walked out. I remember Kathy Eastwood bursting into laughter at this point. Richard Clatworthy and I then stood up and between us made the point that, even if P3E worked, all it would do would create more profit for the company, higher dividends for shareholders and larger salaries for our directors; our members wouldn't gain at all. Mark Packer of APEX then had his turn, repeating the same points. We then stood up in unison, another twenty or so reps, and walked out.

The P3E quality circles went ahead without our involvement. We put out a joint union statement under the banner, 'P3E = Pursuit of Profit at the Price of Employees' and asked our members not to participate. Few did. Alf Gale's vision of Japanisation faded away in less than a year.

Two other developments occurred at the end of the year. In December, TASS and the Association of Scientific, Technical and Managerial Staff (ASTMS) members voted by large majorities to merge the unions, around 78% in favour to 22% against. The new union was to be called Manufacturing, Science and Finance (MSF). During the year our Broad Left meetings were dominated by this issue. ASTMS, on paper at least, was a much bigger union of around 500,000 members distributed across a far broader range of occupations and industries than TASS. There was a good deal of disquiet expressed about such a contrast. TASS was a union of around a quarter of a million members, nearly all of whom worked in the engineering industry. We regarded that concentration as an asset and the source of our militancy. Employers generated a surplus from our labour, a process of exploitation that was not so keenly felt, if at all, in some of the industries covered by ASTMS. Nevertheless, this was a project led by Ken Gill, along with a number of senior TASS officials, and their arguments won the day. Gill's view was that engineering would become the most important sector in the new union and the Broad Left would retain its dominance.

Immediately following the ballot result, the TASS Divisional Councils began a process of internal merger, in preparation for the full MSF merger. In our case, the South West council that incorporated Bristol, Somerset, Devon and Cornwall merged with the one covering Gloucestershire and Wiltshire. Fresh elections were necessary for the interim positions of president and secretary. This was the cause of a major division in the South West Broad Left. The Morning Star communist faction put up Eileen Godfrey as their candidate for president and supported me as secretary. The secretary was the more arduous role, one I was used to, while the president was the figurehead who chaired the new Regional Council meetings. Eileen Godfrey was a member of the faction but without any workplace base. She worked in a small non-union insurance company as a supervisor. Many of us who worked in the unionised plants felt that such people were often union careerists, intent on getting a job with the union without having to experience the sheer hard graft of workplace organising. But she was supported by Derek Perkins and Dave Yeomans, our two main communist officials in the region. Charles Lomas, our token left-wing Labour Party organiser, asked me to stand against her. After a period of contemplation I agreed, though I knew that Derek Perkins, a man I admired and often worked closely with, would be hostile to my candidacy. In the event, the next

Broad Left meeting voted in my favour as so many of its members came from large, unionised plants sympathetic to our main argument. I have to add that Derek Perkins got over this fairly quickly. I believe he was not entirely convinced that Eileen was the right candidate for the role even though it was only a one-year interim position.

Before the year ended, we put together another pay claim for 1988, again based on the Blue Book data. BAe had a new chairman, Professor Roland Smith, who had been touring the media outlets, painting a picture of a company that displayed outstanding performance. You've guessed it, higher sales, record profits, higher share dividends, an "exceedingly strong balance sheet" and so on. We followed his lead by submitting a claim for a 7.5% increase. Management responded with an offer of 3% plus a new incentive scheme paying a derisory £50. We might have been heading for a new dispute were it not for the bombshell that hit us in early 1988.

1988-1991: The jobs crisis

1988 BAe's 'The Way Ahead' and the joint union alternative strategy

BAe, like most other large corporations, established a merry-go-round of senior managers constantly moving positions to generate continual organisational restructuring, or we might say, job cutting. The new managing director of the Dynamics Group was himself replaced at the beginning of 1988 by John Parkhouse. In the first week of March, he announced a major restructuring entitled 'The Way Ahead'. A shortfall in work had been identified as a result of the loss of US contracts, project delays and the MOD's reduction in spending on conventional weapons. Although the Berlin Wall had not yet come down, the period of the late 1980s was that of a new detente between Western leaders and the Soviet President, Mikhail Gorbachev. Many political analysts wrote of the prospects for a 'peace dividend', a shift in government spending from defence to other social priorities. The Thatcher government could only see the potential for spending cuts.

Sir Raymond Lygo, the Chief Executive of BAe, had already announced his intention to cut costs by 30%. By this he meant labour costs. John Parkhouse announced that his restructuring of Dynamics involved the axing of 3,200 jobs at the Filton, Bracknell and Stevenage sites, of which Filton would lose approximately 1,100 initially, potentially rising to 1,400. Moreover, apart from a residual production workforce of 100 to support project design, Filton was to cease its manufacturing activity with most of this moving to Stevenage. This meant the loss of many manual workers' jobs along with TASS production support staff such as test engineers, production planners and so on. In industrial relations terms it meant the loss of the more militant sections of the workforce. The job cuts were to be managed over a period of 18 months, allowing the company to disingenuously claim that there would be no compulsory redundancies.

At the time that John Parkhouse was appointed, he secured the services of a new Personnel Director, Mike Usher-Clark. We subsequently found out that Usher-Clark had developed a reputation for moving around companies and sites managing job losses. Parkhouse seconded him to our Filton site, where, alongside Ernie Peck, he led the redundancy negotiations for management. Usher-Clark was one of the new wave Human Resource Managers, adopting the HR philosophy that assumed that workers shared the same interests as their employers. Ernie Peck by contrast was more of an old school industrial relations manager, hard-nosed but prepared to acknowledge the clash between these different interests. I preferred that.

The Parkhouse announcement did result in one positive development—it united the site unions. At least for a while. We formed a Joint Union Committee (JUC) comprising a representative from each of the newly named AEU (Chris Sims), TGWU (Bill Richmond), Joint Inspectors' Unions (Bob Mead), APEX (Mark Packer) and MSF (myself). This committee was to take overall charge of negotiations for the site unions and to plan an alternative strategy. Initially, I was its secretary and Bill Richmond took on the role of chair. Later, I took over as chair.

Our first position was to formally reject the company's plans. Mark Packer and I proposed that we prepare to move to a 'failure to agree' as soon as possible and then to ballot for industrial action. However, we were faced with a serious obstacle. Management had clearly planned for this possibility and granted Usher-Clark an extremely generous budget to buy off the opposition. The principal instrument was a redesign of the company's Selective Early Retirement Programme (SERP) which comprised a package of redundancy pay and early access to pension payments. It took us some time to establish how the redundancy payments were calculated because management argued that nobody would be made compulsorily redundant and, therefore, they were offering individualised severance pay rather than redundancy pay. As such the unions had no right to access such personal information. This daft position was subsequently overturned when APEX took the company to an industrial tribunal and won.

The problem for us was that the redundancy pay on offer was extremely generous. Comprising two elements, length of service and age of the individual, it was paying as much as four weeks' pay for each year of service for those workers with long service and far more for those with less, so that younger workers were compensated for potential lost future earnings. This meant that some members with lengthy service could walk out with a lump sum equating to two year's pay whilst those with less service could receive as much as eight, nine, ten or more week's pay for each year of service. This was at a time when many redundant workers across the country were receiving little more than the statutory entitlement of one week's pay for each year of service. In addition, there would be no actuarial reduction of pensions for leavers down to the age of 56. That also meant that older workers received large pension lump sums.

It didn't stop there. Management opened on-site job centres with job counselling and were offering to pay for six months' worth of re-training. Courses that were eventually funded included those for HGV driving, motor mechanics, gas installation, plumbing, carpentry, computer servicing, electrical installation, computer software and so on. Grants were made available to pay for college courses, teacher training, and even, in one case, training to become a vicar. This meant that workers in the threatened areas could take as much time off as they wished on full pay during the 18-month period of job cuts to look for alternative employment. And during this time, they could partake in their approved training courses, also on full pay, with course fees covered by the company.

As a result of this, nearly 100 workers applied for redundancy in the first three months of the programme. Many were those in their fifties and sixties who were keen to retire. But more were indicating their intention to do the same at some point, while the re-training on offer was attracting much interest. Understandably, a disproportionate number were workers in the plant's manufacturing areas. And so, when Mark Packer and I proposed a programme of one day protest strikes at the JUC it was met with opposition from the manual union groups. All of us knew we would be faced with compulsory redundancies at some point in the 18-month 'The Way Ahead' programme but in the critical production areas and, to be honest, in some of our own MSF production support areas, we were told it would be almost impossible to secure a majority for action.

We therefore found ourselves in a contradictory position. On the one hand, the JUC unions were determined to oppose the redundancy programme using whatever limited means were at our disposal. On the other hand, many of our members expected us to sit down with management to negotiate the details of the redundancy and re-training package and, indeed, to represent individual members for the many grievances that were likely to arise. We had no choice but to engage with the latter processes, given that there existed no consensus on taking industrial action. But we continued to oppose the redundancies by devising a political strategy that concentrated on alternatives to job losses in the defence industry.

Our strategy of opposition was called 'The Alternative Way Ahead' before it eventually became 'The Alternative Strategy'. Initially, it was based on three core proposals, which did not always sit together coherently but at least allowed us to explore different means of saving jobs. First, we argued that the proposed transfer of weapons production from Filton to Stevenage should be cancelled. Our argument was that by reducing Filton to a smaller design centre with little manufacturing, the efficiencies that are gained by the close liaison between design, development and production would be lost. Moreover, the reduced size and status of the Filton site would render it expendable in further company rationalisations. Second, we argued that many of the jobs at risk at our Naval Weapons Filton site could be transferred to the adjacent Civil Aircraft site. At the time, BAe was proposing to sub-contract millions of pounds worth of Airbus work to the USA. We argued that the company should instead invest in the Filton site and arrange for the transfer of our workers whose jobs were at risk to the new Airbus work. The third part of our strategy was the most radical and over time it came to be the dominant component.

Essentially, we argued that if the bulk of our arms factory was to become redundant, then it should be subject to a conversion to socially useful production. The details of this developed as we involved our members in the process. Our initial argument was that for some years our various managing directors and site directors had been warning us that changes in government defence policy and procurement were likely to have damaging consequences for our members. Not least of these were the effects on conventional weapons expenditure of the £10 billion Trident programme, recent overall defence spending cuts and particularly severe cuts in the Royal Navy's budget. Our position was that it was foolhardy for the company to dogmatically concentrate on a declining market and ask our members to pay for the consequences. Moreover, at a time when BAe and many other aerospace and manufacturing companies were complaining about the lack of skilled engineering workers in the UK, it was senseless to lay off thousands of such workers. Our immediate solution was to convert specific plants that were at risk while, at the same time, defence companies should undergo a gradual wholesale diversification into new civil high technology markets. The initial examples we gave our members and management were wind-turbine electricity generators, telecommunications equipment, commercial computers, electronic office equipment and new transport systems. We noted that our site already had much of the technology and infrastructure for this in our high quality mechanical and electronic engineering areas, our printed circuit board manufacturing centre and one of the UK's most advanced thick film hybrid technology centres.

These were the arguments we put to our members at a number of joint union mass meetings in May. Some of us were fully aware of the notable arms conversion campaign carried out in 1976 by shop stewards at Lucas Aerospace, based on their 'The Alternative Corporate Plan'. Like us, the Lucas unions were fighting job cuts. I was well acquainted with this through my work with the Better Future for Defence Jobs Committee that I had joined a few years earlier, as were some of our MSF reps and members through their attendance at TASS weekend schools in the past. I had also read published work by Mike Cooley, one of the leading activists involved with the Lucas plan. Although media reports at the time emphasised how the Lucas stewards raised the simple moral choice between manufacturing weapons of war or kidney dialysis machines, in fact, many of the alternative products suggested by their trade unionists were very clearly aligned with their existing work and skills. For instance, the development of heat pumps, solar cell technology, wind turbines and new forms of transport technology. This was exactly the alignment that we were seeking at Filton twelve years later.

There was one critical contextual difference between the union campaigns at Filton and Lucas, however. In 1976, the Lucas stewards had the benefit of a Labour government and, in particular, of an ally in Tony Benn, who, at the plan's inception in 1974, was Secretary of State for Industry. We had the Thatcher government which was decidedly hostile to the idea of trade unionists challenging corporate policy. Moreover, we were aware that whilst the political conditions in 1976 were more favourable, ultimately the Lucas management succeeded in carrying out their planned redundancies. Nevertheless, we ploughed ahead. I was very keen on developing the policy, as was the new MSF Joint Office Committee. The two leading APEX reps, Mark Packer and John Milsom—a Militant Tendency member—also strongly supported it as did Charlie Fenwick of the EETPU. Chris Sims (AEU) and Bill Richmond (TGWU) were more sceptical, though for the sake of JUC unity they agreed to go ahead with it.

Actually, on 23rd May, some of us did take industrial action of sorts. Four hundred of our manual and non-manual workers took the day off, filled eight or nine coaches and travelled to London for an impromptu lobby of Parliament. Having suggested to the JUC that we do this, I was the stressed organiser of this lobby. By now I had taken part in a number of TASS aerospace lobbies and the whole operation looked pretty straightforward to me. But the difference was that the others had been run by our national organiser, Chris Darke, with all the resources that head office could offer. At the beginning of May, I spoke to Chris and informed him of our plan. He was horrified at first. His view was that lobbies had to be tightly controlled and the participants had to behave responsibly. Taking hundreds of angry union members to Westminster did not augur well. Nevertheless, he did provide some advice and agreed to book Westminster Hall for the opening speeches. He also agreed, provisionally, to turn up himself to give a speech.

The JUC carried out all preparatory work: coach bookings; handouts for members summarising our alternative strategy; draft letters to local MPs and national figures; and so forth. The hall was booked for 1.00pm and the lobby of MPs was scheduled to start at 2.00pm. We booked the coaches to arrive in London for 12.00 but somehow, on the day, we arrived far earlier, well before 11. If hundreds of trade unionists arrive in London with plenty of time on their hands, there is only one place they will seek. A local pub. At 12.30 we began rounding our members up and it was pretty clear that some had consumed far too many beers. Nevertheless, we managed to pack into Westminster Hall for 1.00pm.

Chris Darke had contacted me the day before to let me know that if he didn't eventually make it then I would have to give the main speech. He didn't arrive so I stood on the main platform and gave a reasonable speech on the key points of our strategy and the necessity of support from politicians and the state.

We then headed for the main Lobby Hall. The JUC had a meeting with Bristol South MP Dawn Primarolo, who had been supportive throughout, and she then took us to meetings with Labour's shadow defence team, including the Shadow Secretary of State for Defence, Martin O'Neill. All were sympathetic to our arguments and explained the Labour Party's developing policy on establishing a defence diversification unit. None of this would impact to any extent on our predicament though. Meanwhile, our members were meeting local MPs, at that time mainly Tories—Michael Stern, Robert Hayward and Jonathan Sayeed. I was later informed that one of these had taken a group on to the Westminster terrace for drinks—not a good idea. One of our MSF test engineers had drunk so much that he came close to falling into the Thames.

Just before we were due to leave the Lobby Hall, who should wander in but Sir Raymond Lygo and Professor Roland Smith, the Chief Executive and Chairman of British Aerospace respectively. Apparently, they were on their way to meet ministers to discuss development grants for Airbus. We had no idea that they were going to be there, and they had no idea that we were going to be. They soon found themselves surrounded by a few hundred of their hostile, and not entirely sober, human resources. Given the condition of our members that day we could see a clear look of panic on Lygo's and Smith's faces. We refused to let them budge until they agreed to meet us at the factory and eventually Lygo disclosed that he was travelling to Filton two days later on 25th May and agreed that he would meet us then.

On the morning of the 25th, Ernie Peck rang me to say that Lygo was locked in discussions with the site directors at the BAWA conference room and no longer had the time to meet us. Seething with anger, I told Peck that if that's the case he would find himself again surrounded within 30 minutes. They relented. But it was not a useful meeting, and I had no illusions to the contrary. A surly Lygo dismissed most of our arguments. He came close to completely losing his temper on the question of arms conversion, growling that it was management who are paid to run companies and that the idea of workers planning and executing policies for factories was extreme left-wing utopianism. The only point he did agree with was that locating design and production side by side was far more efficient than separating them into different sites. This only confirmed our fears that the future of our remaining design function at Filton was at risk.

Our political campaign also focused on local government support. Following JUC appeals to Bristol City Council, Avon County Council and Northavon District Council, we were invited to address the City Council's Economic and Community Development Committee on 27th May. We were indebted to Pam Tatlow for this, the left-wing Labour councillor and leader of the Labour group. By now I had become the JUC's spokesperson on the Alternative Strategy. Following my speech, the committee agreed to offer resources to help the JUC analyse alternatives to the job-loss programme, primarily the argument for arms conversion. We were then invited to put our case to a full council meeting in the main council chamber on 4th June. This date fell in the middle of my union's annual conference, to which I was a delegate. This one was important, a Special Rules Conference of our new MSF union held in Bournemouth. I shall come to this a bit later. Derek Perkins offered to lend me his union car, enabling me to drive up to Bristol for the meeting and then to return to the conference in the evening. By the time I arrived at the council chamber I was pretty shattered. I was greeted by a full house of councillors while the public seating area was packed with our union members, along with a large lobby group of single mothers with their babies. As I looked up at them, I was amused to spot Mike Usher-Clark and Ernie Peck sitting rather uncomfortably in the middle. When called to speak, I walked on to the chamber floor, faced the mayor and proceeded to outline the case for our alternative strategy. When I had finished, I heard a roar of approval from behind, no doubt with the exception of the two personnel managers, and the councillors then proceeded to a debate. The Council voted to condemn management's 'The Way Ahead' redundancy programme and asked the company to review its plan to end production at the Filton site. Importantly, it also agreed to offer funding and research facilities to aid us in expanding our alternative plans.

When I emerged from the council building, I gave interviews for local BBC and HTV television news bulletins and to local radio. I should have mentioned that by now I had become a regular fixture on local TV and radio; a week did not go by without my having to provide an interview for one or more of the media outlets. Usher-Clarke told me at one meeting that I had become the de facto media spokesperson for BAe and I should be careful with what I had to say. I ignored this, of course. Initially I found the interviews pretty nerve wracking but after a while I got used to them and eventually took them in my stride. The trickiest one came straight after the job losses were announced, when ITN interviewed me at the main gate for a live national news bulletin. They told me I would be asked a question about the job losses and that I had precisely 47 seconds, no less, no more, to answer. Which I did! The funniest interview I gave was with, I think, Radio Bristol, when I was asked to participate in a live three-way discussion on alternatives to job loss in the South West. This was to take place after the news at 8.20am one weekday morning. Eileen had just left to take the girls to school and I was late, still having a shower. When I heard the phone ring, I rushed downstairs to answer it and was horrified to hear the programme producer saying I would be live in two minutes. I had completely forgotten I had agreed to this but proceeded to offer my wise thoughts on how to oppose job losses whilst standing naked, dripping wet.

At this point in the arms conversion campaign, the JUC had drawn up the initial alternative strategy document and then held mass meetings to secure membership endorsement. The next stage was to involve members directly in drawing up more detailed alternative plans. The JUC designed a questionnaire for a membership survey. This was essentially a skills audit and a call for ideas on alternative products. For this we drew on our knowledge of how the Lucas shop stewards prepared their Alternative Corporate Plan. Our questions requested information on the following: what tasks our members performed at Filton; their skills and experience; equipment and technology used; types of BAe products worked on; other products worked on outside the aerospace industry; ideas on alternative civil products using existing site technology that their skills could be utilised on; and alternative civil products that could be produced if retraining and plant investment was supported with appropriate resources. The surveys were circulated to all members and, although I no longer have a record, the total number of responses was high, sufficient for us to compile a complete list of skills of approximately 1,500 technical staff, 400 mechanical craft operators, 160 electrical craft operators, 120 inspectors and 450 clerical workers.[16]

16 JUC News, Bristol Dynamics Joint Union Committee Newsletter, October 1988.

We were able to collect a long list of members' suggestions for alternative products. These included: semiconductor research and development for civil electronics markets; microchip manufacture; optical underwater components; electronic control and monitoring equipment; commercial computers; amplifiers; antennae and satellite TV dishes; telecommunications equipment of various types; commercial satellites; cable systems; information and electronic mail systems; computer software packages; factory robotics technology; plant process machinery; microwave components; consumer electronics goods; electrical control panels; pneumatic compressors; refrigeration plant; printed circuit board design and manufacture; wiring looms for the aerospace and marine industries; electronic medical equipment; optical equipment; automated test program design; CADAM equipment; chemical process equipment; motorised vehicle design; hydraulic systems; structural design services; communications analysis; air traffic control equipment; ceramics technology; low cost motorcycles; radio frequency devices; technical publications; domestic appliances; new energy systems; generators; desulphurisation plant; combined heat and power technology; offshore exploration and seabed equipment; locomotive design and production; rail mounted maintenance equipment; vehicles and technology for the proposed Bristol light rail system.[17]

We were thrilled with these responses. We then selected some of the suggestions for further work by interested members and these were developed into more detailed and costed product plans, incorporating the skills and technologies that would be necessary. Eventually the results of this survey would be fed into our work with Bristol City Council sponsored researchers towards the end of the year.

In July, John Parkhouse, the managing director of the Dynamics Division, came to Filton specifically to receive the JUC's Alternative Strategy. Parkhouse sat alongside Mike Usher-Clark, Ernie Peck and other managers while I presented our Alternative Strategy paper with my JUC colleagues. The meeting lasted nearly three hours. After my presentation, Parkhouse went through the different proposals and rejected each in turn. The main item of arms conversion which by now we had reluctantly changed to 'planned diversification' on the advice of Derek Perkins, Dawn Primarolo and others, was more positively received. Parkhouse actually admitted that in theory it made sense. This made a change from every other senior manager we had met, who

17 Ibid

regarded it as anathema to the core interests of BAe. However, he argued that the company had tried diversifying many times in the past and had been unable to make any profit. Our counter-argument was that if that were true then management needed a radical shake-up. Moreover, as it was regularly on its hands and knees to government requesting state aid for various arms projects, it should try the same for alternative civil products. But, of course, our arguments got nowhere. In a summary of the meeting for a JUC newsletter I wrote that,

> BAe will continue to grow by buying other companies rather than investing in existing plants. Its main objective is to create money and maximise profits through any means possible rather than remain a UK manufacturer of aerospace systems. BAe will continue to secure orders and will manufacture in any country where exchange rates and labour rates are favourable. It is a company that is being run totally in the interests of its shareholders and no longer in the interests of its British workforce.[18]

In the meantime, we were still attending endless negotiating meetings with senior management, including a number of works conferences with the EEF, attempting to improve and clarify the complex package that the company was offering redundant workers. At one of these works conferences on 5th September, the company brought in external caterers to provide the union side with a luscious banquet, including a crate of twelve bottles of wine. This was their misguided way of trying to buy us off. In the lunchtime adjournment, the EETPU convenor, Charlie Fenwick, got a couple of his mates to wait outside the window of the meeting room. Eleven bottles of wine were then passed over and never seen again!

One success, after intense lobbying, was an increase in the number of jobs being offered to our members at the adjacent Civil Aircraft Division plant, mostly for Airbus work. Another was to reverse the company's astonishing decision to pay women less severance than men. This old-fashioned patriarchy was typical of certain types of BAe manager, a good number of whom had armed services backgrounds. Due to their initial secretive approach to sharing information on the severance terms, we had no clear evidence that women were being

---

18 JUC News, Bristol Dynamics Joint Union Committee, 2 August 1988.

underpaid. However, as each member began receiving their severance pay offers, they reported these to their union reps and we were able to construct a fairly accurate matrix. Amongst other things, this showed a clear pattern of sex discrimination. The issue became a cause for heated arguments at two works conferences held in the spring and summer. When the JUC, with the help of an industrial tribunal ruling, finally forced management to disclose the severance pay criteria, they had to hand over two contrasting sets, one for men the other for women. We then secured the help of the Equal Opportunities Commission who advised us that the company was making payments that were unlawful under the Sex Discrimination Act, the Equal Pay Act and also European legislation. It was not until September that management conceded equal terms for women. Even then they only agreed to apply this change from September, refusing to compensate women who had left the company since March. An MSF member, Margaret Daly, was affected by this and agreed to take her case to an industrial tribunal, supported by our union. At the last-minute management backed down and sent Margaret a cheque for over £8,000 corresponding to the extra amount she should have received. They did likewise for all other women leavers.

At this point I shall return briefly to MSF's Special Rules Conference at Bournemouth in June. The objective was to approve a rule book for the new union. Like any rules' revision conference, the agenda was packed with many motions and amendments. There were two issues that stood out, however. The first, and probably most important, concerned the funding of branches. Under the system adopted by ASTMS, all branches received annual funding amounting to 10% of branch membership subscriptions. Within certain limits, branches could spend this money in any way they wished. Money that was not spent during any year would remain in branch accounts, where in many cases it would stagnate, untouched for years. By contrast, the TASS system of funding was centrally controlled. TASS branches were paid small budgets each year to allow for small scale officer expenses, local donations to other groups of workers in struggle and branch affiliation to organisations such as the Anti-Apartheid Movement, Amnesty International and so on. The vast majority of union income was controlled at the centre. It wasn't just the Broad Left that supported this. Most members who were aware of the system believed that money was best controlled by national and regional officials and was the better guarantee against individual corruption and wasteful spending.

The second issue was the method of electing delegates to the annual conference and the size of the conference itself. The ASTMS system was based on branches electing conference delegates directly, making for conferences in excess of 1,000 delegates. The TASS approach involved a smaller number of delegates, elected from district conferences and divisional councils. Our belief was that this approach was more efficient and, paradoxically, more democratic. For us, the real debates took place at the divisional level and at local Broad Left meetings while, in the main, the annual conference acted to endorse the outcomes of these internal discussions. We feared that the ASTMS approach, if adopted for the much larger MSF union, would result in an unwieldy conference. Due to time constraints, it was likely that too many decisions would be referred back to the National Executive Committee, thus denying delegates any meaningful input into policy-making. A larger conference would also be very expensive.

Neither of these items appeared on the agenda for the first day. But there were plenty of motions and amendments to discuss. I have to say that I, and many of my TASS colleagues, felt embarrassed by what happened. We were outnumbered by the ASTMS delegates but on practically every vote where disagreements emerged during the debates, the TASS delegates—the vast majority of whom were Broad Left members—voted as one, whereas the ASTMS delegates were hopelessly split. And they lost every vote. I was sitting next to Ron Warren, the convenor at Rolls Royce's Filton plant. Ron was a great negotiator and very astute politically. As the day developed, he kept whispering in my ear that this couldn't go on, that there'd be a reaction at some point. Ron was very close to the Rolls Royce ASTMS convenor, Alastair Fraser, who was a member of the ASTMS National Executive. They met up a few times during that day to discuss what had occurred. I went for a drink with Ron that evening and he called it a bloodbath, as apparently did many ASTMS members. He also said that Alastair Fraser and his NEC colleagues had been attending private meetings with key ASTMS activists and that they were confident that things would change the next day.

On this next day the method of branch funding was up for discussion. I have to say first of all that I and my TASS colleagues were shocked by the apparent manifestations of the ASTMS funding system. A good number of their delegates brought their wives or partners to Bournemouth, which we heard was paid for by branch funds, that is, membership subscriptions. During the evenings, many seemed to be eating at the best restaurants, again with all expenses paid. We were not used to anything like this. The previous evening, we had attended the traditional Broad Left conference meeting where the Assistant General Secretary, Barbara Switzer, had disclosed that we were inheriting a huge ASTMS debt with far fewer paying members than we had assumed. So much for the financially secure new union. The imperative, therefore, was to win the vote on branch funding. But something had changed by the next day. The voting patterns of the ASTMS delegates were transformed into something more coherent and unified. It had become a bipartisan conference and now the Broad Left was in the minority. We lost the vote on branch funding and a good number of other votes as well. We would have lost the vote on the future size of conference as well, had the item not been withdrawn for certain technical and legal reasons.

With the new union in place, the Broad Left changed its name to the Unity Left, in an effort to attract ASTMS activists. But this proved fruitless. What happened at that three-day conference was in reality a harbinger of the decline and fall, not just of the Broad Left and its dominant Morning Star Communist Party faction, but more importantly of the transformation of a unique left-wing and at times militant white-collar engineering union into something more moderate and indistinct that appealed to a larger mass of individualistic professional workers. By this I mean the attitude of the typical MSF member began to change. No longer "what can we achieve by acting together?" but instead, "what can the union do for me?". As the decade drew to an end and the Filton plant began losing its manual workforce, together with a good number of our more militant white-collar sections, I began to experience management policies that were aimed at supporting just such attitudes.

By now, back at Filton, I had switched roles from secretary to chair of the MSF Negotiating Committee. Richard Clatworthy, the previous chair, had decided to throw in the towel and take advantage of management's retraining offer. Kathy Eastwood took on the role of secretary. In the summer we held a leaving event for Richard at a Bristol No 4 Branch meeting. Derek Perkins was there to give a farewell message. Tim Kenneally from the Test Department suddenly turned up with a large leaving present wrapped in CND gift paper. When Richard opened it he found a Sea Wolf missile inside. Derek Perkins went a deathly shade of white. Reader, do not be too concerned. The missile did not carry a live warhead, it comprised only the outer shell of the missile and had been used as a display model. Tim had smuggled it out of the main gate and at the end of the meeting he was asked to smuggle it back in again.

While most of our activity was focused on the job loss crisis, we also spent much time negotiating a 1988 pay settlement and completing the flexitime agreement which came into operation at the end of the year. Simultaneously, my work with the MSF Regional Council had expanded considerably. Following the Special Rules Conference in the summer, the union established new Regional Councils, much larger than our old Divisional Councils, comprising delegates from the old ASTMS and TASS from across the South West. Ron Warren and I had garnered much support from the many large aerospace plants in the region to stand as president and secretary. There were no objections from the ex-ASTMS delegates. I was duly elected Regional Council Secretary at the end of the year. This also meant I had to attend all sub-committees. For many weekday evenings I now had to be present at the Finance and General Purposes Sub-Committee (essentially, the executive committee), the Political Sub-Committee (discussions on our input into Labour Party politics and our own political campaigns) and the Education Sub-Committee which covered various union education initiatives, especially the regular weekend schools. In addition to this, I was a delegate to the Bristol Trades Council, another weekday meeting commitment.

Then there was my ongoing Labour Party activism. I was elected MSF delegate to the 1988 Labour Party Conference at Blackpool. This was the year Tony Benn stood against the leader Neil Kinnock. The result was an overwhelming vote in favour of Kinnock. Despite the protests of the minority Broad Left members amongst the MSF delegation, our block vote went with Kinnock. In the summer, my Henleaze Labour Party selected me as their candidate for the City Council elections. This was also a lost cause. For years, the Labour Party vote had come in third, well behind the Liberals and winning Tories. I secured the help of Kathy Eastwood and Frank Tamlyn in knocking on doors and irritating the local Tory bourgeoisie. In the event I received 629 votes, 14% of the total, just behind the Liberal Party candidate. The Tory won with over 2,000 votes.

Had I won that election it would have caused a local political earthquake. It would also have caused an earthquake at home. I was working full time on union work during the day and on many evenings and weekends. Inevitably, this level of involvement was increasingly straining our marriage. I had become obsessed with the labour movement and the objective of reaching the golden shores of socialism. But I knew, deep down, I was kidding myself. Democratic socialism was far out of our grasp, slipping away from the Labour Party's agenda for change, and Thatcherism seemed hegemonic. I was never a revolutionary in the sense of supporting a violent overthrow of the capitalist system. I preferred more peaceful means of change. I suppose I was a radical social democrat. I think I still am. Nevertheless, union and party activism was like a drug and I couldn't let go. Meanwhile, Eileen was at home much of the time, feeling increasingly isolated. Many evenings when I came home from work I would do as much of the childcare as I could, but then I would be out again, off to yet another evening or weekend meeting. Eileen told me recently that she also believed she was suffering from mild post-natal depression. Her solution was to get out of the house and try something new. She made the decision to return to full-time employment by commencing a three-year training programme to become a specialist registered nurse in learning disabilities. It was the beginning of a long and fruitful career for her. As the saying goes, every cloud has a silver lining.

For this we needed childcare and a new house. In August 1988 we moved to a four-bed house in Claremont Avenue, Bishopston. We employed a child-carer from Turkey, Deniz, initially as an au pair. For this, Deniz was required by her agency to attend English language classes at the local Brunel college. However, she didn't really enjoy these (though she did warm to Bristol's nightlife) so she ended the au pair arrangement but stayed with us for a time and provided childcare cover when neither Eileen nor I were at home.

One final memory of 1988 was my participation in a Channel 4 documentary entitled the Gilded Cage, made by an independent film company, Forum, based in Bristol. I remember one of the staff working on this was named Nancy. Little did I know at the time but her partner was Theo Nichols, later to become my PhD supervisor and a good friend. The film focused on the arrival at Filton of Hewlett Packard, a powerful American multinational company. The company opened a large computer design and manufacturing plant just a quarter of a mile from the Naval Weapons site. This caused quite a media stir since Hewlett Packard was well known for its anti-union stance, employing new wave management strategies aimed at winning the hearts and minds of its employees to such an extent that their commitment to management and the company was total. Many thought this was an exercise in brainwashing. Channel 4 was equally interested in the impact it might have on the densely unionised aerospace complex located nearby. Chris Darke, my old national aerospace organiser, had left the union. His replacement was Tim Webb, who I got to know quite well given his record in supporting arms conversion. Forum had invited Tim to take part in the film and he persuaded Kathy Eastwood and me to join him. I have to say I greatly enjoyed myself. We were taken to the factory and filmed as the company's human resources manager gave a guided tour. We were then filmed taking part in a heated discussion on the merits of union representation with the manager and later with some employees. I still have a copy of this film and recently took another look at it. Apart from my dodgy moustache, I think I came out of it pretty well. We certainly gave them far more flak than we received in return. Later I was told by the film's producer, Lee Cox, that the human resources manager had left the company one month after the film was televised and nobody knew of his whereabouts.

1989: The campaign continues

1989 began with a major national industrial dispute in engineering—the renewed CSEU campaign for a 35-hour week. The dispute developed during the latter half of 1988 when the EEF and its constituent companies, especially BAe, took a hard line in rejecting union proposals to gradually reduce the working week. Negotiations broke down at the end of the year and the CSEU commenced a dispute strategy centred on all-out strikes at selected engineering sites, backed up by a £4 per week levy of union members across all sites. Many of the sites selected were in the aerospace sector, including BAe plants at Chester, Preston and Kingston. We held mass meetings at Filton and, despite all our other difficulties and the realisation that non-manual workers were unlikely to gain from the dispute, our members responded well to the call for a levy. The dispute ended messily in the early Spring of 1989 without a national agreement. Nevertheless a 37-hour week was established in many plants, thus bringing manual workers into line with the non-manuals. This was because individual companies signed up to a reduction of two hours to avoid the risk of further strikes, including, eventually, BAe. The dispute signalled the end of a role for the Engineering Employers Federation in industrial relations as its constituent companies resigned, determined to avoid any further national disputes.

Our campaign for arms conversion moved up a gear following my presentation of the Alternative Strategy to the City Council in June 1988. Councillor Pam Tatlow, who I have to say was fully committed to our cause, authorised funding for a team of researchers to work with the JUC to produce a detailed report on the BAe job losses and our union strategy. John Lovering, a political geographer at the School for Advanced Urban Studies, Bristol University, was assigned lead researcher to work with staff in the City Planning Department's research section. He already had an interest in arms conversion policy and had previously published in that area. Not long after the research commenced, John Lovering came on site to discuss the JUC's strategy and access our membership survey data. He also met senior management but only on their condition that the project did not have a 'political' tag. In this respect they were reacting to both our involvement and the input of the more left-wing Labour councillors. Nevertheless, I met up with John a good number of times, including socially in pubs, to help him progress the report.

The final report entitled, *BAe in Bristol. What Future?* was published in January 1989.[19] The JUC was very pleased with it. The report provided analysis of the extent to which the Bristol economy was dependent on the aerospace industry—almost 30% of manufacturing employment—and how the Filton job losses were a casualty of a set of changes in markets, government policy and management policy. Crucially, it criticised BAe management's current strategy, arguing that a reliance on military markets did not promise long term security. At the same time, it fully supported our Alternative Strategy, emphasising the high technology bias of the JUC's alternative product plans. It stated that, *"No other recent proposals from a British defence plant have included such technologically sophisticated ideas"* (italics in original). We made sure that copies of the report were circulated widely around the plant.

Our management was less impressed. We understood well that a single local authority report would have little impact on 'The Way Ahead' redundancies or indeed on BAe's future strategy. Nevertheless, the JUC used it in continuing to press for our arms conversion objectives and our approach generated intense management hostility at times, far greater than did any of our conventional industrial disputes. Essentially this

---

19 Bristol City Council, University of Bristol, CSEU, BAe In Bristol. What Future? January 1989.

hostility boiled down to their objection to any worker or union input into corporate strategy, what used to be called industrial democracy.

On the 12th January, I walked into Avon House, Bristol, to address a full meeting of Avon County Council. My speech promoted arms conversion at Filton and requested support for this along with council involvement and financial support for the recommendations of the City Council's *BAe in Bristol* report. The council was controlled by Labour and my requests were supported. The *Evening Post* reported the following day that my speech was applauded by Labour members only.[20]

The *BAe in Bristol* report also provided meat for our wider political campaign. In compiling it, John Lovering had liaised with Phil Asquith at Sheffield City Council. Phil was one of the original activists behind the Lucas Alternative Corporate Plan. The outcome of this was that the report's main recommendation was to establish a National Diversification Unit involving a country-wide network of local authorities, trade unions and employers. To further this, Pam Tatlow, John Lovering and I travelled to Westminster in February to meet again with Martin O'Neill, Labour's Shadow Defence Secretary, and also Bryan Gould, the Shadow Trade, Industry and Environment Secretary. I was impressed with Gould. Of all the national politicians I met during this campaign his support for arms conversion and our Alternative Strategy seemed the sincerest. Eventually, after losing the party leadership election to John Smith, he left the party in 1992 and moved to New Zealand.

Back at Filton the atmosphere on the office and shop floor darkened further when the site managing director, Dennis Atkin, announced to the JUC that the senior management at Stevenage, now headed by yet another new managing director, Norman Barber, had requested a review of staffing levels across all Dynamics Division sites. A new 'The Way Ahead' would be announced shortly. To make matters worse, our Printed Circuit Board manufacturing facility, which had succeeded in diversifying into commercial contracts with the likes of British Telecom, would close in 1990. Forty-five workers would lose their jobs. By now we realised that 'The Way Ahead' pointed only to the dole office. In the middle of April, we were called in again and given notice of an additional 357 job cuts at Filton. The severance package and training support would be extended until the end of 1990. We immediately registered a failure to agree. At the ensuing works conference, Atkin sat

---

20 *Evening Post*, 'Unions' plea to help save BAe jobs', 13 January 1989.

BAe in Bristol. What Future? Report.

alongside the representatives of the Engineering Employers Federation to pour scorn on our demands for arms conversion. He repeated that BAe had in the past attempted to diversify into civil markets but did not find it sufficiently profitable. Its strategy was to focus on the business it knew best and if the market for that was shrinking then so must the workforce. I was close to despair at this point. We all knew management would be coming back for more at some stage, inflicting death by a thousand cuts, while our membership was becoming weaker by the day and losing the will to fight back.

Many of us took part in yet another London rally and lobby of Parliament on 26th April. This was a national BAe affair, organised by the Confederation of Shipbuilding and Engineering Unions. Again we met Dawn Primarolo and other Labour politicians, but by now I felt we were going through the motions. This was no reflection on Dawn. At this stage in her career, she was still a member of the Socialist Campaign Group, and following the approach of her old boss, Tony Benn, would always put herself out to meet and support workers in struggle. I could not say the same for some of the other senior Labour politicians I met, however. The worst example was Gerald Kaufman who, in 1989, was the Shadow Foreign Secretary. I was again an MSF delegate to the Labour Party Conference in Brighton in September. I met up again with Dawn and she arranged a private meeting with Kaufman. As Dawn and I sat waiting for him in a small hotel room he eventually turned up looking as if he'd just hopped off a billionaire's yacht. There he was, tanned and dressed impeccably in cream chinos and a dazzling blue polo shirt. He sat down and listened to what I had to say and said he agreed fundamentally with our arguments for conversion, or diversification as he preferred to call it. He then gave a firm commitment to including Labour's support for such arguments in his conference speech the following day. When the time came, I sat expectantly with my MSF colleagues. All I can remember of it was the complete absence of any reference to diversification, or conversion, or anything remotely linked to the plight of our members.

By now, anyone reading this might assume that I was alone in leading our Filton campaign for arms conversion. This was not so. I was certainly the main protagonist and public face of the campaign. But most of the JUC unions played their own roles in securing and maintaining support from their members. Within my own union we had many reps arguing our case, together with individuals such as Ed Tily on the negotiating committee, and a new young career-based engineering rep named Doug Roberts, who took charge of converting our ideas of product alternatives into costed project plans. When I say that most of the JUC supported us, there were two notable exceptions. Chris Sims of the AEU and Bill Richmond of the TGWU were tentatively on board in 1988. But eventually they decided to come off the JUC and concentrate on negotiating better redundancy terms for their members. They announced this in the summer while I was on holiday. When I returned, I accepted their decision but thought it was done in a cowardly way.

I suppose that if I had been more realistic, I would have concluded that it was inevitable that weaknesses would develop within our own union organisation and in our relations with the other site unions. As time went by our members were leaving us. A good number retired early with the severance package (many in their 50s), younger members took up the offer of retraining and tried their hands at self-employment in a variety of trades such as carpentry, plumbing, electrical work and so on, while others succeeded in transferring to the Civil Aircraft Division to work on Airbus. One of our few successes was the application of public pressure to persuade our managers to request Airbus management to take on more of our redundant workers.

During the remainder of the year, I carried on giving speeches and talks to various interested parties with the aim of building political support for a national conversion strategy. John Lovering and I led a special debate at the Bristol Trades Council and then did the same at the Yeovil TC. This latter meeting was dominated by trade unionists from Westland Helicopters and it was gratifying to receive warm support for our arguments. I travelled to Manchester to give a talk to trade unionists at the Mechanics Institute and again this was well received. I remember receiving a truly critical grilling from a meeting organised by the Green Party in Bristol. Their line was that our members, by working in the arms industry, were essentially immoral. My counter-argument was that if any man or woman desired a decent skilled engineering job in Bristol then they would have little option but to find employment in the industry at some point. They could not exert the labour market choice that these Greens supposed. Moreover, my core argument was that if we wanted to change the defence sector's domination of the UK's manufacturing industry then the dynamic of change had to come from workers within the plants as well as from political leadership at the top.

Nevertheless, we did need supportive political leadership and the campaign suffered a major blow when, in the late autumn, leading figures from the District Labour Party centre-left- and right-wing factions combined to oust Pam Tatlow as leader of the City Council Labour group. The coup was headed by Phil Gregory, the Regional Secretary of the TUC, along with other local TUC figures and Doug Naysmith, a local councillor who would later become a Bristol MP. There were two politicians in Bristol who provided us with much needed assistance in our campaign. They were both women, Dawn Primarolo and Pam Tatlow. Pam's removal meant the impetus behind the creation of a local authority network supporting a national diversification unit was lost.

With MEPs at the European Union Arms Conversion Conference, Brussels. Barbara Switzer is third from the right.

Towards the end of the year, I received an invite from Barbara Switzer, the Assistant General Secretary of TASS—and now MSF—to accompany her to the headquarters of the European Union in Brussels to take part in a large conference on arms conversion, organised by groups of MEPs and researchers. I met Barbara at Heathrow along with another convenor from BAe Warton where we boarded an Airbus. Like many aerospace workers, this was the first time in our lives we had flown. I found it quite a scary experience. We encountered a good deal of turbulence and with my seat adjacent to the wings I was constantly worrying that the flapping wings would inevitably come off. In the event, we landed safely.

Barbara Switzer had a reputation for being somewhat stern and aloof. But in 1983 she was the first woman to rise to the height of Assistant General Secretary in any union and to achieve this in such a male dominated movement she was necessarily tough and hard-headed. I got on with her very well and found her warm and supportive of everything we were trying to achieve as activists. The event itself was held at a huge conference centre in the EU complex and full of various European politicians, researchers and bureaucrats. There was also a large team of translators so that with the aid of headphones we could listen to all the contributions in perfect English. I made a well-received contribution on the central importance of worker participation in any attempt at arms conversion. This was not easy because I had to speak slowly, leaving gaps between each sentence, so that the translators could do their work. When I had finished, I sat back and thought about how I had started off my working life as a shy young apprentice in a nondescript Wiltshire town and yet had somehow developed into someone who could stand up and give a speech to a full house at the European Union headquarters. Life is strange.

By the end of 1989, most of our negotiating committee members had gone, as had half of the Joint Office Committee. We had little problem filling the vacancies with new representatives but the political complexion of our workplace organisation changed. Lost from the negotiating committee were Kathy Eastwood, Richard Clatworthy and Phil Harrison, all good Broad Left members. Kathy was a particular loss because she was also a very committed branch secretary and active in the region. She joined Bristol City Council as a researcher in the housing unit. Our new negotiating committee comprised me as chair, Mike Parker, Ruth Gilchrist (our women's rep), Doug Roberts, Tim Porter (barely out of his teens and looking the spit image of a young Frank Tamlyn) and Lawrence Smith from the Drawing Office.

1990: Human Resource Management

Our MSF activists were not the only ones to change in this period. The Naval Weapons Filton plant appointed a new managing director, Steve Hollingsworth, to replace Dennis Atkin. The head of Personnel, Mike Usher-Clark moved on to other BAe sites, presumably to continue his work on job cuts. By now plant rationalisations were a constant feature of life at any BAe plant. He was replaced by Jim Palmer who transferred from the Preston site and was appointed as our new Head of Human Resources. Not long after he arrived, Hollingsworth invited me over to his office. I was wary about this because I would never attend any formal meetings with management on my own. I took a colleague with me, I think it was Mike Parker, to listen to what he had to say. What he did say was that in his opinion, the world of work was far more individualised than previously. Many workers, and particularly white-collar workers, were more interested in pursuing their own careers and looking after themselves than relying on the trade union collective approach. In short, he felt that there was not much of a role left for trade unions at Filton. We didn't really want to engage with this nonsense. Mike and I sat there glaring most of the time and let him know that we fundamentally disagreed. Not long after this, Jim Palmer called us over to his office for an informal chat, as he put it. This didn't last long either. He wanted to share his view that Mike Usher-Clark's policy of offering severance terms that were well in excess of the legal minimum was crazily expensive. As was the retraining budget. He was going to put an end to it when The Way Ahead programme ended in the summer. We left the meeting convinced that more redundancies were on the horizon.

It became clear to us that the old style of confrontational management was being replaced by something softer but more pernicious in many respects. These days, people call this 'partnership'. For example, a new, more junior human resources manager named Ivor Pope began attending union negotiating sessions. He was known for having done some form of work previously with Bristol City Football Club and he had a habit of addressing us as if he were coaching a group of footballers. For example, I remained Andy but Ruth Gilchrist was 'Ruthy', Martin Pearce, the new AEU convenor became 'Pearcey' and the new APEX rep Nigel Phillips became 'Nige'. I hated this. It was all part of his attempt to draw us into his merry company team.

In policy terms, this new human resource management style became a challenge during our 1990 pay negotiations. As I had done for a number of years now, I drafted a pay claim based on a range of economic factors: how our Filton pay settlements had been falling behind settlements in comparable aerospace plants; how the cost of living was on the rise at around 8%; increases in profits, share dividends, etc; and the predictably high annual pay rises enjoyed by our directors, which Sir Raymond Lygo and Professor Roland Smith had been publicly defending, using the argument that British directors are paid less than their European counterparts. Our counter argument was that if that were true then the same also applied to our members' salaries. I had recently acquired a report on employment in the European aerospace industry compiled by the European Metalworkers Federation. This established that average staff pay at BAe was, in real terms, only half the level paid by German aerospace firms such as Dornier and well below others such as Aerospatiale, Fiat and Fokker. I greatly enjoyed doing this type of work because I knew it irritated our management negotiators and helped stir up the membership.

We submitted an MSF claim in early January for a 15% general increase, along with a 35-hour week. Management replied with a 16.5% offer spread over three years, that is, 5.5% each year. Three quarters of the difference between the rate of inflation (RPI) and 5.5% would also be paid in 1991 and 1992. Our response was to reject the offer on the basis that it was far too low and that we were not interested in long term deals during periods of high inflation. The management response gave us quite a jolt. The pay offer would no longer apply to our career-based engineers, who were by now the dominant group on site. Instead, for them, a new performance related pay system would be introduced. This put us in a very difficult position.

As I have explained earlier, although we negotiated on behalf of the career-based engineers, this was done without official union recognition being granted. The company turned a blind eye to this because, to be frank, it made the management of pay settlements less complicated and time consuming. But now they had decided to adopt a more individualised approach.

Our response to this development was complicated by our antipathy towards the company's merit pay system. This was a system that was both secretive and discriminatory, whilst its budget ate into the final general pay increase that management was prepared to offer. When we were confronted with management's decision to operate performance related pay (PRP) in the career-based areas—effectively the loss of negotiations in those areas—we were faced with a dilemma complicated by the fact that, although PRP constituted a threat to our collective approach to determining pay, it was, in principle, a much fairer system than merit pay. I say fairer because the criteria adopted to make payments were transparent, negotiable and widely understood. Our dilemma was that if we allowed management to divide us in the way proposed, then our areas of influence through union recognition, post 'The Way Ahead' job losses, would be greatly reduced. The alternative was to accept PRP but on the basis that it was union negotiable for all staff groups. Nevertheless, if we were to go down that route, we risked alienating many of our members for whom collective pay determination was the raison d'être of union membership. And all the time in the background was the knowledge that after 18 months of living through mass redundancies, our members had little appetite for a fight.

After a number of lengthy JOC discussions, the Negotiating Committee, with great reluctance, agreed to meet management to propose a one-year deal with an additional union negotiated PRP element applied to both job-based and career-based areas. As a result, the hated merit pay system would be abandoned. We took this to a mass meeting of members on 12th February and our position was endorsed. We then held a series of intense negotiating meetings with management, led by Ernie Peck, which continued through to April. The matter was settled on 5th April at another mass meeting. The agreement was that MSF would negotiate an annual pay increase every year to be applied to both job-based and career-based areas. In addition, we would negotiate a new PRP scheme, again applied to both job-based and career-based areas. This would include performance criteria, methods of staff appraisal, frequency and consistency of appraisal, new pay structures, extent of typical distribution of PRP, and application of both an equal opportunities policy and an effective appeals procedure. The annual pay increase would be incorporated into the PRP system so that every member of staff would receive, as a minimum, the annual increase.

Anyone reading this might wonder why we were so concerned about these developments. The outcome had been the continuance of annual pay bargaining, de facto management recognition of our right to negotiate for career-based staff and the replacement of a secretive merit system with a more transparent PRP system, over which we now had some influence. Our worry was that PRP was the thin end of the wedge, the first stage of a creeping individualisation of employment relations at the plant. Or, at the least, that eventually the annual pay increase would diminish compared to the individual PRP element. In the event, as we shall see, a further jobs crisis made all of this irrelevant.

During the year the JUC continued its campaign for arms conversion. The inaugural MSF annual conference took place in Bournemouth in May, with over 800 delegates. I moved a motion in support of arms conversion and managed to get on to the front page of the *Morning Star*. *The New Worker*, the weekly newspaper of the New Communist Party of Britain published a short interview with me at the conference. A few weeks later I gave them a more extensive interview to which they devoted nearly a whole page. I seemed to have become a magnet for fringe left-wing papers. Later in 1991, I was the subject of a full report in *The Worker*, the paper of the Communist Party of Britain (Marxist-Leninist) after I had given a speech and answered a string of difficult questions at the Bristol branch of the NUT, the teachers' union. The paper said I dealt very clearly with criticism from some quarters.[21]

On 23rd October, I spoke at a public meeting on Arms Conversion at Transport House, Bristol, organised by the Better Future for Defence Jobs Committee. I shared a platform with Bill Morris, then the TGWU Assistant General Secretary—subsequently elected General Secretary in 1992—and Dawn Primarolo. The meeting was packed and I was very pleased with the lengthy question and answer session that followed. On 11th November, I again travelled to Brussels, this time with Tim Webb, our national aerospace organiser, to participate in another large arms conversion conference at the European Union Parliament building, where I again made a contribution reporting on our Filton campaign. The conference was organised by the Socialist Group of MEPs. At the main conference meal, Tim and I shared a table with Ron Todd, the General Secretary of the TGWU and Jack Dromey, Harriet Harman's partner and TGWU national organiser for the defence sector. I really enjoyed discussing my experience at BAe with Ron Todd. Unlike a few national union and Labour Party figures I had come across, he was in no way condescending or pompous and treated me like an equal.

A couple of weeks later Barbara Switzer asked me if I would be interested in meeting Alan Clark, the Conservative Minister for Defence Procurement. I was uncertain of the merits of this but I thought it might be an interesting experience. Alan Clark was one of the best-known Tory ministers at the time because of his unconventional behaviour and views. He was famously described by the Tory Chancellor Norman Lamont as "the most politically incorrect, outspoken, iconoclastic and reckless politician of our times." Switzer and I met him in his palatial Whitehall office. We walked in and he greeted us by waving at two empty chairs as he lay back on his with both feet perched lazily on his desk. A nervous young civil servant sat nearby, waiting to take notes. We spent around an hour with him discussing the problems of the aerospace sector and our arms conversion solutions. The surprising thing about this meeting was that he agreed with the idea of conversion and he seemed sincere. His view was that it would never happen because the quality of management in aerospace was such that they lacked the

---

21 *The Worker*, British Aerospace must live, Vol.23, No.24, 8 July 1991.

wits and skill to organise it. This was not dissimilar to the contempt for old guard public school British managers often expressed by Tony Benn while in office.

The year ended with a visit to Germany in early December. I travelled to Münster with Derek Perkins and some fellow trade unionists from the Portsmouth Naval Dockyards. This was yet another conference on arms conversion, hosted by the German trade union IG Metall. We spent much time discussing our experiences with trade unionists who had come over from the Bremen dockyards in northern Germany. We also observed a works council meeting in operation. It was interesting though frustrating to hear that even with their works councils, which allowed trade union officials greater influence over company policy than did British management, arms conversion initiatives had not really progressed any further than ours. Still, this was a very pleasant trip. During the whole weekend our hosts plied us with endless pints of German lager, notable for neither sending me to sleep nor giving me any trace of a hangover. Strange. Also, we were given immense amounts of meat to consume. I wondered if this was the secret behind Germany's superior football teams.

1991: Redundant

Nineteen ninety-one was the year it all ended. It started badly and got steadily worse. In January, Ernie Peck arranged a special meeting with the MSF negotiating committee to report on a decision about our claim for a workable equal opportunities policy. I assumed that this was a meeting to finally sign the agreement. You may remember that we had submitted proposals for a detailed policy back in 1986, following the company's announcement of its own risible policy which amounted to just one sentence. The data they subsequently provided showed very low levels of employment of ethnic minority workers and an almost complete absence of women in management roles. Since then, it had been a very slow process, taking almost five years, but we gradually developed a usable policy through a good many negotiating sessions. The draft policy covered areas such as the training of management and staff, an overhaul of recruitment practices and interviewing procedures for both external and internal vacancies, transparent criteria for promotion and the regular monitoring of recruitment and promotion outcomes through plant-wide data collection.

It took us a long time to get management to accept monitoring. It took even longer for them to amend the main policy statement, which eventually read, "that no job applicant or employee receives less favourable treatment on the grounds of sex, marital status, race, colour, nationality, ethnic origin or disability." One sticking point was disability which management refused to concede, on the basis that the company would have to invest in structures that allowed access to buildings. We did manage to embarrass them sufficiently to change their minds finally. Where we failed was with sexual orientation. It was that issue that held the policy up for so long. We were still in the era of Margaret Thatcher's Section 28 legislation, which banned teachers from promoting the acceptability of homosexuality. I tried various approaches to persuade management to add sexual orientation to the policy. Conventional equality arguments did not work. I assumed that some of the management negotiators sitting opposite were probably Christians. I knew that one, I cannot remember his surname, a relatively new recruit to the Personnel Department, was planning to leave the company to train to become a vicar. I regularly scanned newspapers to find quotes from the more liberal Church of England leaders who supported gay rights. I would then read these out to the meetings. But they refused to budge and we had to agree to omit it or otherwise lose the whole policy.

When we started work on this policy in 1986, Kathy Eastwood and I led the negotiations. After Kathy left in 1989, I threw myself into it, devoting much time and energy to securing a favourable outcome. I knew that no site in BAe had established such a policy and that it was unlikely that one existed anywhere else in the aerospace sector. I was finally going to achieve something lasting. In January 1991, Ernie Peck sat down opposite the negotiating committee and informed us that BAe's senior management in London had changed its mind and would no longer endorse the draft policy. Negotiations were over. My face must have looked a picture of dejection because when I eventually looked up, I could see that even Peck felt sorry for me. He also looked highly embarrassed. From that point on I knew that the game was up and I had had just about enough of fighting a constant losing battle.

On 21st March, the JUC was called in by Steve Hollingsworth and Jim Palmer to be told that a further 1,300 staff were to be made redundant, including nearly 700 graduate engineers. From a peak of 4,700 workers at the beginning of the 1980s, a rump of around 600 would remain. We

Detta, Frank Tamlyn, Eileen and Jess at the London march, 26th March 1991.

had already been given advance warning of a pending restructuring exercise across all BAe sites but we did not expect this. I was livid. I told Hollingsworth that this was his fault, that we had predicted such an outcome in 1988 and that if management had accepted our Alternative Strategy, we would not be in such a dire situation.

Five days later another CSEU-led London march and lobby of Parliament took place. This involved all BAe sites across the country, including union members at Rover and Royal Ordnance, acquired by BAe in 1986 and 1987 respectively. The turnout was large with whole families joining in. Eileen, Jess and Detta took part too.

Following this, the JUC then attended a stream of negotiating sessions and works conferences with senior management, including trips to the divisional headquarters at Stevenage. Again and again, we argued the case for our Alternative Strategy but it was clear that once again management was not interested in arms conversion or even small-scale diversification. As far as our side was concerned the meetings were mere exercises in point scoring.

We also held a number of mass meetings. I clearly remember the first of these. I had to read out some of the details of what the company was proposing. This included the number and different types of jobs that were going. I also had to disclose that, unlike with 'The Way Ahead' redundancy programme, we would be given little more than the statutory minimum notice of redundancy, one month following a three-month consultation period. Moreover, the severance terms were to be significantly reduced while the retraining budget for redundant workers was slashed. I looked up at the front row as I was speaking and found a man with tears streaming down his face. This was a very uncomfortable moment.

On 22nd April, teams of managers were called on to interview each worker and tell them of their fate. In my case, I sat opposite a senior Stevenage manager who had driven to Filton for the pleasure. He rather nervously read out a standard statement informing me that I had been selected for redundancy with a leaving date in the middle of May. I sat stony faced throughout without saying a word. When I returned to the union office, I prepared a press release condemning the company's actions. The final paragraph read,

> MSF Convenor, Andy Danford, said that "this is a grim day for the city's aerospace industry. Every constructive union initiative to save jobs has been rejected out of hand. And now the company is cynically attempting to sack the cream of its workforce in the cheapest and crudest way possible".[22]

I rang Eileen after this and told her the news. When I arrived home Jess and Detta ran to the door and gave me a lovely hug. The following day, Ivor Pope rang me to say that the *Evening Post* had sent him a copy of the release and the company was considering dismissal. I laughed and said, "that would be a first, sacked twice in two days." I didn't hear about it again.

On 21st May, what was left of the JUC unions—now comprising new inexperienced stewards from AEU, APEX, EETPU and myself for MSF—held a workplace ballot for industrial action short of a strike. This would comprise overtime bans, go slows and a work to rule. The intention was to place pressure on management to improve the redundancy terms. This was really too little, too late. Many of our members had already left the company or transferred to the Civil Aircraft Division or were absent from work seeking alternative employment, as was their right.

22 Press Release, BAe Dynamics Joint Union Committee, 22 April 1991.

Two minutes each seals the fate of 1,300 people
BAe: The crunch

Workers line up to hear who is to go

TRADE unionist Andy Danford, who led the fight to save 1,300 jobs at British Aerospace's guided weapons factory at Filton, near Bristol, lost his own job yesterday.

He was one of the first of hundreds of staff to be officially told he was being made redundant because of the cut-backs in Government defence spending.

Steve Eyres

Andy Danford

Pete Warren

Nichola Hulin

The rest are expected to learn their fate today ... and it means some of the best technical brains in Britain are set to join the dole queue.

A mass meeting is expected to be held on the site tomorrow, by which time everyone of the 2,100 workers should know their fate.

All workers are being called in by their departmental bosses and told whether they are to be kept on or made redundant.

They have waited four weeks since the company had first announced the job losses to see who will be kept on and each of them is allotted two minutes to learn their fate.

Mr Danford, chairman of the site's joint Shop Stewards committee and convenor for the biggest union there, the MSF, said: "I leave at the end of July."

Mr Danford, aged 39, who has worked at BAe Dynamics for 12 years, and is married with two girls aged ten and 11, added: "I was half expecting it.

"The real shock for all those who are being made redundant will come the day they leave the factory.

"They know there are no jobs to go to.

"What has really upset people today is the crude way in which the management has told them that they are going."

Mr Steve Eyres, aged 46, who has been with the company 11 years said

"As I see it this is the end of Dynamics," said Mr Eyres, of Conygre Grove, Filton, who immediately rang his wife with the bad news.

Mr Steve Johnston, aged 31, from Bradley Stoke, turned up for work wearing a black tie to mark the "black day at Filton".

But he was told his job was secure for the time being.

He said: "I feel very sorry for all my colleagues who have been told they are going. There are no jobs."

One wife whose husband had yet to learn of his future with the company, looked tense and apprehensive.

"My husband has been here six years and I've been here three," said 22-year-old Nichola Hulin, whose own job is secure.

"We've got a big mortgage and we've only been married 10 months," she said.

"If he is told to go, I suppose the redundancy money would keep us going for a while."

Pete Warren, 59, said he didn't feel too bad.

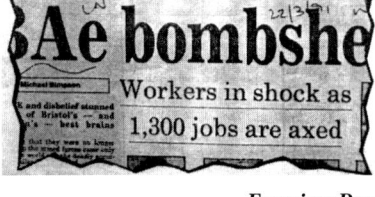

Evening Post, 22nd April 1991.

In the event, 274 members voted in favour, 207 against, 179 were offsite and the remainder did not vote. MSF members were the only group with a majority in support of action. We decided we had an insufficient mandate and all that was left was to continue our efforts to resolve the many members' grievances arising from the severance and training on offer. We did succeed in securing a greater number of vacancies on the Airbus project at the Civil Aircraft Division plant next door, totalling around 300.

I had one more task to complete. The merit pay system that I have described had paid additional salary increases to white-collar staff each year until its replacement by performance related pay in 1990. Around half received an increase every year, another quarter every two years, and the remainder rarely or never received a rise. I joined the Standards Department in 1979. I received a first merit rise in 1980 and received them again in '81 and '82. In 1983 I became a TASS union rep and also

Branch Secretary. From that point onwards my merit pay rises came to an end. My one PRP rise in 1990 was the bare minimum. I knew that in some companies, such as Rolls Royce, MSF had informal agreements that guaranteed the full-time union convenors an average of the total per cent merit increases paid each year. My good friend Ron Warren, the Rolls convenor at Filton, had warned me that such arrangements sometimes resulted in individuals standing for election for the wrong reasons or, indeed, in changing their behaviour towards management. The alternative was to remain a martyr. And that was my position. However, once I had received formal notification of redundancy, I decided to take up a grievance against management of pay discrimination on the basis of trade union activity. It started with my departmental manager and ended up with the HR Department, where I faced Malcolm Fiddler. I was accompanied by Mike Parker. After a long argument I was awarded a 4% pay increase although Fiddler refused to concede that this was for discrimination. I had had enough by now but I took the money since it boosted my severance and pension.

My final attendance as a delegate at the MSF annual conference was in May. I moved a motion condemning the ways in which the exploitation of agency and fixed-term contract workers was undermining the rights of permanent staff. Derek Perkins informed me that Ken Gill had told him that my speech was one of the best he had heard at these conferences. This cheered me up a bit, even though I knew it was all coming to an end.

I drafted one more JUC newsletter on 15th July. It provided a guide to state benefits. We were in the middle of a severe economic recession. I also had one final media commitment. The BBC had asked me to take part in a *Panorama* special on the subject of recession and redundancy. The presenter was the BBC's Economics Editor, Peter Jay, James Callaghan's son-in-law and ex-ambassador to the USA. He and his cameramen came to our house in the morning and filmed me getting the girls' breakfast. He then interviewed me there, and again at the Industrial Museum on the harbourside where shots were taken of me walking around the mock-up of the Concorde flight deck. I found it all a bit intrusive, though I did get in my pennyworth on alternatives to job loss. He drove me home in his ancient Jaguar saloon car after we found a volunteer to help us get it started with jump leads.

I was due to leave in the third week of July. By then, and with the help of John Lovering, I had managed to get a place at Bristol University to study the final two years of a three-year BSc in Sociology. My completed

Open University modules had given me an exemption on the first year.

I walked out of the plant for the final time on the morning of Monday 22nd July. As the song goes, I was in a melancholy mood. I crossed the road and looked back at the old buildings but there were no tears of regret, more a sense of relief. The whole union experience had been a wonderful political education but the final two years were demoralising. At home, Eileen might have worried about the money situation but she was much happier. We fell in love for a second time.

Epilogue

My final activity in the arms conversion campaign was to travel to Moscow and Kiev on 15th December 1991. John Lovering put me on to this. I went with a delegation of the British Peace Assembly at the invitation of the Soviet Peace Committee. The group of eleven comprised trade unionists, peace campaigners, members of the Campaign Against the Arms Trade, academics and local councillors. When there, we split into two groups. I was a member of the arms conversion group. We met a number of senior Soviet officials, generals and industrialists, including Mikhail Bazhonov, the President of the Arms Conversion Committee under President Yeltsin. We also toured a military computer factory that had been converted to civil production. Most interesting was an interview with Boris Kagarlitsky, a sociologist, noted socialist dissident and a member of the Moscow City Soviet.[23] In the context of a pending economic collapse, Kagarlitsky argued for a radical left-wing version of the Roosevelt New Deal. It didn't happen. The centre of Moscow clearly bore the scars of the failure of the August coup against Gorbachev. We left on 24th December, the Soviet Union's final day.

I completed my sociology degree in 1993, a PhD in 1996 and became an academic. I was appointed professor at UWE, Bristol, in 2005. As for others in this account:

Eric Stott still helps to run the old Swindon folk club previously run by Ted Poole and his wife.

Frank Tamlyn retired and became a car park attendant at Frenchay hospital, where he consistently refused to collect parking fees from the less well-off visitors.

Kathy Eastwood rose to a senior role at Corporate Services, Bristol City Council. Ten years of austerity drove her to early retirement in 2020. Mike Parker became Kathy Eastwood's partner. They had two kids. Mike remained a calibration and maintenance engineer at a small specialist engineering business in Bristol until he retired.

Richard Clatworthy started a business as a self-employed plumber. After this failed in the recession of the early 1990s, he moved to his native Cornwall and became a salesman for a plumbing wholesaler.

Phil and Dawn Harrison and family moved to a hamlet in northern France after buying and refurbishing an old house. They have lived in

---

23 I have since been reliably informed that Kagarlitsky's political position has moved towards the far right, embracing Russian nationalism. He is often found in the company of fascists and red-brown third positionists.

different parts of France ever since, making a living refurbishing old properties.

Ron Warren retired in the mid-1990s. He moved with his wife to Portugal. He died there some years later.

John Lovering became a professor and eventually moved to Cardiff University. Around ten years ago he moved to Turkey with his partner.

Dawn Primarolo became Paymaster General in Tony Blair's Labour Government and Minister of State for Public Health and later Minister of State for Children and Young People under Gordon Brown. She is now Baroness Primarolo.

Pam Tatlow became the Chief Executive of MillionPlus (the association for modern universities in the UK).

Barbara Switzer stood for the election of General Secretary of MSF in 1992 after Ken Gill retired but was defeated by the Blairite Roger Lyons. In 1992 she joined the General Council of the TUC and in 1995 was President of the Confederation of Shipbuilding and Engineering Unions.

Chris Darke left MSF in 1992, immediately following Barbara Switzer's defeat, and became General Secretary of the British Airline Pilots' Association (BALPA). Derek Perkins, Charles Lomas and Dave Yeomans all retired from MSF not long after Barbara Switzer's defeat. Charles Lomas became a regional official of the Radiographers Society in his native Liverpool. Dave Yeomans married a Russian academic and moved to Moscow.

Abbreviations

ACAS	Advisory, Conciliation and Arbitration Service
AEEU	Amalgamated Engineering and Electrical Union
AESD	Association of Engineering and Shipbuilding Draughtsmen
AEU	Amalgamated Engineering Union
AGM	Annual General Meeting
ANC	African National Congress
APEX	Association of Professional, Executive, Clerical and Computer Staff
ASTMS	Association of Scientific, Technical and Managerial Staffs
AUEW	Amalgamated Union of Engineering Workers
AUEW-TASS	Amalgamated Union of Engineering Workers (Technical, Administrative and Supervisory Section)
BAC	British Aircraft Corporation
BAe	British Aerospace
BAWA	British Aircraft Welfare Association
BBC	British Broadcasting Corporation
BFDJC	Better Future for Defence Jobs Committee
BICC	British Insulated Callender's Cables
BSI	British Standards Institution
CAD	Computer-aided design
CADAM	Computer-aided design and manufacturing
CAMRA	Campaign for Real Ale
CND	Campaign for Nuclear Disarmament
CP	Communist Party
CSEU	Confederation of Shipbuilding and Engineering Unions
DATA	Draughtsmen's and Allied Technicians' Association
EEC	European Economic Community
EEF	Engineering Employers Association
EETPU	Electrical, Electronic, Telecommunications and Plumbing Union
FTO	Full Time Official
GCE	General Certificate of Education
GLC	Greater London Council
GEC	General Electric Company
GW	Guided Weapons
HGV	Heavy Goods Vehicle
HNC	Higher National Certificate
HRM	Human Resource Management
HTV	Harlech Television

ISO	International Organisation for Standardisation
JOC	Joint Office Committee
JUC	Joint Union Committee
MEP	Member of the European Parliament
MOD	Ministry of Defence
MSF	Manufacturing Science and Finance Union
NEC	National Executive Committee
NHS	National Health Service
NUM	National Union of Mineworkers
ONC	Ordinary National Certificate
PRP	Performance Related Pay
PSG	Product Support Group
RAF	Royal Air Force
RPI	Retail Price Index
SWP	Socialist Workers Party
TASS	Technical, Administrative and Supervisory Section
TGWU	Transport and General Workers Union
UWE	University of the West of England
TUC	Trades Union Congress
YTS	Youth Training Scheme

Bibliography

Bristol City Council, University of Bristol, CSEU, *BAe in Bristol. What Future?* January 1989.

Bristol Evening Post, 'Unions' plea to help save BAe jobs', 13 January 1989.

Bristol Evening Post, 'Ask the workers about the future of Westland', 2 January 1986

JUC News, Bristol Dynamics Joint Union Committee Newsletter, October 1988.

JUC News, Bristol Dynamics Joint Union Committee Newsletter, 2 August 1988.

JUC Press Release, BAe Dynamics Joint Union Committee, 22 April 1991.

R. Newman and J. Slack, 'Usher's [sic] of Trowbridge: disappearing one brick at a time',
https://boakandbailey.com/2020/05/ushers-of-trowbridge-brewery-history/
Accessed 5 November 2020.

B. Parkin, '*The Broad Left in TASS*', International Socialism, No 74, January 1975.

I. Pollock, 'Child Poverty: Wales is the only UK country to see an increase',
https://www.bbc.co.uk/news/uk-wales-48259327.
Accessed 4 December 2020.

swindonweb, 'Planes, Trains and Automobiles', http://www.swindonweb.com/index.asp?m=8&s=116&ss=402.
Accessed 3 November 2020.

TASS News and Journal, July/August 1985

TASS Bristol No 4 Branch Newsletter, 1986 Annual Wage Claim, 1985.

TASS Bristol No 4 Branch Newsletter, 1987 Pay Claim, October 1986.

TASS Bristol No 4 Branch Newsletter, 6 April 1987.

P. Taylor and Peter B., '"Subterranean Worksick Blues": Humour as Subversion in Two Call Centres', Organization Studies, Vol.24, Issue 9, November 2003.

Today, 18 April 1987.

B. Wootton, Incomes Policy, London: Davis-Poynter, 1974.

The Worker, 'British Aerospace must live', Vol.23, No.24, 8 July 1991.

Acknowledgements

I am greatly indebted to my good friend Mike Richardson who inspired me to write this memoir, who read and commented on the first draft and offered valuable support. I am also grateful to Richard Musgrove, who co-ordinated the production process and was always on hand to provide guidance and to answer my many queries, and proof-readers Barbara Segal and Ralph Openshaw. I would like to thank my friends Theo Nichols and Bob Carter for reading the first draft and urging me to get it published. I must not forget Frank Tamlyn, a great trade unionist and friend of mine for over 40 years and I thank him for providing clarifications whenever requested.

I thank my two daughters Jess and Detta, who were young girls during the 1980s, for providing the impetus for this work. I wanted to give them an understanding of what they have lost, of what working lives were like at a time when trade unions were stronger and more influential than today. Finally, I owe so much to Eileen, the person who will always come first. I am very grateful to her for proof-reading earlier drafts of this memoir. But I must add that she suffered and persevered with my obsessions throughout the period I write about and she has done so with love ever since.